LANGUEDOC

James Bentley

LANGUEDOC

Photography by Charlie Waite

SALEM HOUSE
TOPSFIELD MASSACHUSETTS

Photographer's note
Charlie Waite would like to thank Jessamy Waite
for her superb navigation.

Library of Congress Cataloging-in-Publication Data
Bentley, James, 1937—
Languedoc.
Includes index.
1. Languedoc (France)—Description and travel—Guide-books.
2. Languedoc (France)—Description and travel—Views.
I. Waite, Charlie. II. Title.
DC611.L292B46 1987 914.4′04838 86-31447
ISBN 0-88162-277-X

Text © James Bentley 1987
Photographs © Charlie Waite 1987

First published by George Philip,
27a Floral Street, London WC2E 9DP

First published in the USA by Salem House, 1987
462 Boston Street, Topsfield, MA 01983, USA

Printed in Italy

Half-title illustration **Montcalm, half-way between
Aigues-Mortes and Saint-Gilles-du-Gard.**

Title-page illustration **The forests around Fronsac
coming to life in spring.**

Contents

To Joanna and George

Introduction

One summer as I toured the Languedoc the sun was so strong that I gave up sightseeing every afternoon and headed for the local *piscine*, the open-air swimming pool that no self-respecting town in the Midi can do without. Then I decided to make for the Mediterranean, arriving at the ancient port of Collioure one blindingly hot afternoon. The colours of the landscape were also hot – red fields, violent green vineyards, the deep blue of the sea. These reds, blues and greens transformed twentieth-century art, for in 1905 the painter Henri Matisse came to Collioure, looked at the sea and shore and suddenly exploded into violent colour. The critics called him a wild beast. Fauvism (from the French *fauve*, or wild animal) was born. In 1905 Fauvist paintings were described as the 'blotches of a child dabbling in a box of colours'. Today we recognize what Matisse painted at Collioure in 1905 and afterwards as masterpieces.

The whole of the Languedoc is rich with such delights. Its cuisine is often based on a combination of fruit and meats that foreigners might suspect could never agree with each other – until, that is, you taste them and are entranced. Languedoc cuisine is for me the culinary equivalent of Fauvism, foods juxtaposed with apparent violence which turn out to be utterly delicious. Roquefort, that blend of sharp salty veins and rich sweet cheese, can be succulently matched with, say, a white Listel wine in a mouth-watering combination. The Languedoc is not a region producing many wines that can be dubbed truly great, but all its wines are exceedingly drinkable and frequently boast a distinctly powerful flavour. Hilaire Belloc, remembering an inn and a girl called Miranda in the high Pyrenees, also remembered that the wine tasted of the tar (presumably because it contained too much tannin); but he meant it as a compliment.

Part of the extraordinary variety of the Languedoc derives from the simple fact that this region is vast: a land of vineyards, torrential rivers, seaside resorts with ancient ports concealed at their hearts, oak forests and mountain scrub. Stone-built villages vie in charm with ancient Roman cities. Catalan Catholics and stern Huguenot Protestants were both sheltered by this immensely varied region. Sometimes known as Languedoc-Roussillon, it covers over 30,000 square kilometres in southeast France, and takes in eight *départements*: Lozère, Tarn, Gard, Hérault, Aude, Haute-Garonne, Pyrénées-Orientales and Ariège.

The Languedoc has a distinct character all of its own, quite unlike anywhere else in France. It has its own language, the *langue d'oc*, and the way of life of its fiercely independent people has strong undercurrents of violence and savagery which would never be found in Normandy or the Loire.

The famous Cistercian abbey of Fontfroide.

A crumbling Languedoc pigeon-house.

From the tenth to the twelfth century it nurtured those remarkable lyric poets, the troubadours, and fostered outstanding romanesque architecture and entrancing medieval cities. To this day its poetry, its food, and its buildings embody a distinct regional flavour. This is also a sensationally beautiful part of France, with spectacular landscapes ranging from the gorges of the Tarn in the Cevennes National Park to the Pyrenees in the south and the windswept vistas of the Petite Camargue.

The Pyrenees, 430 kilometres long, divide France from Spain. The redoubtable Freya Stark described them as 'wilder than the Alps'. Even so the Pyrenees never stopped the French armies venturing into Spain and Spaniards venturing back. For centuries part of the Languedoc was ruled by Spain, and its culture still reflects a strong Spanish influence.

The Duke of Wellington described the Pyrenees as 'the most vulnerable boundary of France, probably the only vulnerable one'. In recognition of the strategic importance of this area, Louis XIV had the frontier fortified. Whichever way you drive towards Spain you find that his brilliant military engineer Vauban has been there before you, strengthening the walls of the frontier towns. Coming back into France from across the Pyrenees, you appreciate just what Louis and Vauban achieved.

Military men play a major role in this book. Commanding a force of some 40,000 troops, as well as his celebrated elephants, the Carthaginian general Hannibal crossed the Pyrenees into southern France in 219 BC on his way to the Alps. The legacy of the period of Roman rule is particularly striking and includes Europe's greatest Roman aqueduct, the Pont du Gard,

Spanish influence is clear in the tiles and ironwork of this window at Arles-sur-Tech.

'the most impressive, the most permanently enormous' antique monument in Europe, as Hilaire Belloc put it.

Until the seventeenth century invasions never ceased. In the early fifth century the Vandals, driven from Germany by the Huns, sacked parts of the Languedoc. The Visigoths followed, making Toulouse the capital of their kingdom. In the conflict between Muslims and Christians in the Middle Ages the stability of the Languedoc was constantly threatened by Saracen invasions, while major crusades against the Muslims were mounted from here, some led by the pious King Louis IX (St Louis as he is called). Not content with crusading against Muslims, the orthodox Christians also mounted a savage crusade in the Languedoc against the heretics known as Albigensians, totally wiping them out.

This region of France also has strong English connections, stemming from Edward III's claim on the French throne in 1337. Edward's son, the Black Prince, was particularly brutal in trying to uphold English claims here, levying harsh taxes and burning cities that dared oppose him.

Religious bigotry broke out again in the late sixteenth century, when the Languedoc welcomed Protestantism. Caught up in the Wars of Religion, frightful outrages were committed by both sides.

In the next century powerful local lords set themselves up against the French monarchy, and were savagely put down. Then the monarchy managed to regain the parts that had been annexed by Spain, and Louis XIV ruthlessly centralized the administration of the whole region, attempting to stamp out its unique character and language. He also revoked the measure of toleration that had been granted to Protestants, provoking a bloodthirsty war in the Cevennes.

The French Revolution left its mark, with many churches demolished and others transformed into temples of reason. But much survived. There are superb examples from every period of French architecture in the Languedoc.

I have followed the routes given in this book many times, and they will give you a tour of the Languedoc if you follow them to the letter. But you need only to stray a few kilometres from my paths to discover secret nooks and crannies and unknown bits of paradise for yourself. Wherever you go in the Languedoc you feel you are breaking new ground.

I know of no other part of France where travel so magically intermingles spectacular scenery, history, totally unexpected architectural masterpieces, hilltop villages and ancient brooding cities. The Languedoc is an unspoilt tourist's paradise.

At the end of his little tour of France Henry James sat on a bench in a French park. He thought over all the places he had visited, and as the light faded the vision of the things he had seen became not less but more distinct.

The vision of my many happy times in the Languedoc became more distinct as I wrote this book. I have to thank Audrey who always came with me, Charlie Waite, for being such a superb collaborator, and Pauline Hallam who so kindly put the resources of the French Government Tourist Board at my disposal.

James Bentley

Paul Riquet's elegant Canal du Midi, near Béziers.

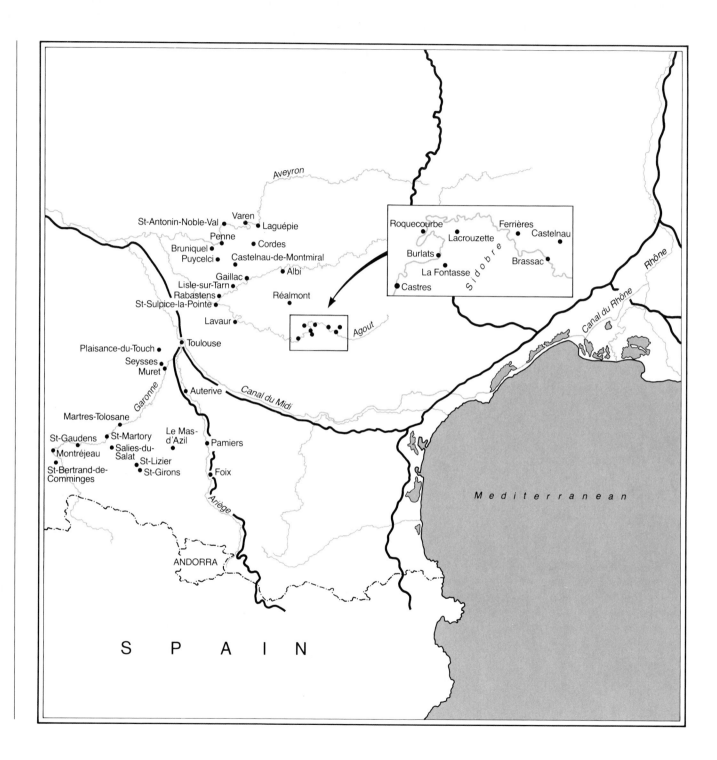

1
The Lands that were Cathar

Toulouse – Gaillac – Cordes – Albi – Castres – the Sidobre – Lavaur – Saint-Gaudens – Saint-Bertrand-de-Comminges – Foix – Pamiers

I made my first visit to Toulouse because of a totally unexpected meeting at the Gare Austerlitz in Paris. Sitting on a porter's trolley after breakfast one summer morning, waiting for a train to take me to where I live in southwest France, I spotted a young blond couple walking hand-in-hand along the station forecourt. As they came nearer I was amazed and delighted to see that the girl was my elder daughter.

With student rail reductions, they were journeying to Toulouse. Would I like to come with them? In an instant I had telephoned the rest of my family in the Dordogne. They got on the train at Gourdon. That evening we all sat in Toulouse drinking garlic soup and eating omelettes made *inter alia* of sausages. Even the most hard-pressed father can afford to buy his family *tourin toulousain* and *omelette occitane*.

The excellence as well as the cheapness of Languedoc food has helped persuade me to return again and again to this magical region of France. Both the history and the landscape are romantic. The River Garonne tumbles down the mountains of the central Pyrenees, winds its way through the great plain south of Toulouse, and makes a huge loop just outside the city before turning west. In AD 107 the tribe known as the Volces Tectosages rebelled against their Roman allies here, and lost.

The Volces had lived on the high ground above the river. The Romans now developed a new town on the left bank, at a point where the Garonne is fordable, which they called Tolosa. The Latin poet Ausonius, who was later to govern Gaul, studied here in the fourth century. In his verse he praised Toulouse as his beloved nurse, already, as he wrote, 'a city of rose red brick'.

Today the city of Toulouse describes itself as the capital of the Languedoc. Between 419 and 505 it was the capital of the kingdom of the Visigoths and after that of the duchy of Aquitaine. Toulouse prospered and was much coveted. Both Henry II (in 1159) and Richard the Lionheart (in 1188) besieged the city in their vain attempts to hold onto their French inheritance. In the early thirteenth century Count Raymond VI defended the city against the Albigensian crusade, mounted to crush the so-called heretical Cathars and led by the formidable Simon de Montfort.

Raymond favoured the suspect religion. The future Louis VIII wrested Toulouse from him in 1215; Raymond recaptured his capital two years later; and in 1218 de Montfort himself took up the siege. A woman flung a rock at him from the city walls, de Montfort's skull was smashed and he died.

An unexpectedly fortunate result of his death was the start of Toulouse University, for Count Raymond was obliged as part of his penance to maintain four theologians, two grammarians, two canon lawyers and six masters of arts in the city at his own expense for ten years. By the end of the century Toulouse had passed peacefully into the hands of the kings of France, through the marriage of Raymond VII's daughter to Alphonse de Poitiers, brother of Louis IX. By now, however, the city was being run by eight democratically elected consuls, called *capitouls*, after whom Toulouse town hall – the 'Capitole' – still takes its name.

The Capitole is an excellent spot to begin a tour of Toulouse. Oddly enough, this magnificent building dates only from the eighteenth century. Until then Toulouse was administered from several buildings scattered throughout the city.

In 1727 the *capitouls* commissioned Guillaume Cammas to build a town hall with a splendid classical façade some 128 metres long, boasting eight huge red marble pillars, one for each *capitoul*. Cammas was an architect with respect for the past. Behind his façade of red brick and white stone he retained the twelfth-century keep, which now serves as the tourist office. The noted restorer of medieval buildings, Viollet-le-Duc, got his hands on it in the nineteenth century. It now displays an upper storey that a distinguished architectural historian has justly described as one of Viollet-le-Duc's disconcerting fantasies. I like it very much.

Guillaume Cammas also incorporated a courtyard designed in part by Nicolas Bachelier in the mid sixteenth century. Inside this courtyard, over Bachelier's monumental doorway, is a marble statue of King Henri IV. High up on the walls are plaques with the coats of arms of long-dead lawyers. And in the centre of the courtyard a flagstone declares:

> The Duke
> of Montmorency
> was executed here on
> 30 October 1632.

As Henry James observed, the history of Toulouse is saturated with blood and perfidy. Montmorency, governor of Languedoc, had joined Marie de Médicis

and Gaston d'Orléans in a conspiracy against Richelieu and Louis XIII. Montmorency lost.

When Henry James visited the city in 1882 he was shown the butcher's knife that allegedly severed Montmorency's neck. I failed to track this down, but did manage to see the Hall of the Illustrious inside the town hall, which Henry James did not. (It was covered in scaffolding at the time of James's visit.) A superb example of the architecture of the mid nineteenth-century Third Empire, it boasts splendid frescoes tracing the history of the city, including Benjamin Constant's *Entry into Toulouse of Pope Urban II* and Jean-Paul Laurens's recreation of the death of Simon de Montfort.

Walk through to the massive place du Capitole, which hosts a weekday market and offers a fine choice of cafés. One of the privileges granted to a *capitoul* was the license to add a tower to his house, and the finest is in the rue Gambetta (No. 1) which runs southwest from the square. Jean de Bernuy commissioned Mérigo Cayla to build it for him in 1504. Both the entrance and the stone decorations of the brick tower are still in a graceful gothic style. But twenty-six years later, when Jean commissioned Louis Privat to build him a palace here, he demanded one similar to the renaissance châteaux that rich merchants and courtiers were now building in the Loire.

De Bernuy's wealth from woad and banking was such that he stood as guarantor to the emperor Charles V when he was obliged to ransom King François I of France from the Italians. Here in 1533 de Bernuy entertained the monarch, who came in person to thank him.

From here rue du Taur leads through numerous second-hand bookshops – quite properly, since part of the university is at No. 56 (its tower is the oldest in the city, the remains of a twelfth-century fortress). In nearby rue du Périgord is the municipal library, with a superb collection of ancient manuscripts and incunabula. Follow rue du Taur to the astonishing church of Saint-Sernin.

I first came to Saint-Sernin, Toulouse, to find a corpse: that of the only English king to be declared a saint. But the moment I saw this sensational red brick building, I forgot the initial reason for my visit. The basilica of Saint-Sernin at Toulouse is one of the greatest churches of the western world, built to commemorate a remarkable holy man.

Saint-Sernin is dedicated to St Saturninus, who brought Christianity to Toulouse in the third century and was martyred here. The first bishop of the city, Saturninus preached in Spain as well as France. At Toulouse he built a small church, provocatively sited next to the pagan temple.

Subsequently the temple oracles ceased. The pagan priests blamed the Christian bishop. One day they hauled Saturninus into their temple and insisted that he sacrifice to the false gods, or they would appease them with the saint's own blood. Saturninus replied, 'The sacrifice of your immortal souls pleases your gods more than the sacrifice of your bullocks. In no way can I fear such deities, for they themselves shiver with fear in the presence of a Christian.'

This was too much for the pagan priests, who tied Saturninus by his feet to a bull, and then goaded it into a rage. The bull dragged the saint until his skull was broken, his brains spilled out and the rope broke: blood and perfidy.

Two Christian women bravely rescued Saturninus's body. And where the rope had broken the church of Notre-Dame-du-Taur was built, its name (deriving from *taureau* or bull), like that of the rue du Taur at the head of which it stands, commemorating the brute beast that killed the saint. Built in 1360, this church had a remarkable influence on ecclesiastical architecture throughout the Midi, its west façade in particular – a strange fortified wall with hanging bells – being copied again and again in this region. The interior is bare and spare, with a sixteenth-century choir on a romanesque crypt and fading wall paintings (both fourteenth- and nineteenth-century) peeling from its walls.

The body of the saint was soon moved, down the street so to speak, as far as the great romanesque basilica. This is built in the form of a Latin cross, with no fewer than five naves, on the site of an earlier much smaller church that covered the saint's earthly remains. The whole is crowned by an octagonal tower, five storeys high, itself topped by a spire.

The choir of Saint-Sernin was completed in almost record time, begun around 1075 and consecrated by Pope Urban II in 1096. (He was in France to preach the First Crusade, and the sculpted altar he consecrated is still here in Toulouse, dating incredibly from the sixth century.) Then the nave was built. Finally the tower was added in the early thirteenth century, the two upper storeys finished around 1250. The differences between the bottom three and the top two storeys are quite marked: for example, the bottom three have round arches, the top two arches pointed like a medieval mitre; yet the whole is deliciously satisfying.

Go in by the south door (known as the Porte Miègeville, because it formally gave out onto the central, or 'median' street of the city). Although the present doorway was built in 1535, the remarkable carving above it dates from 1120. It shows Jesus ascending to heaven – with the help of six angels, two who are carrying him on their shoulders and four more who speed him on his way. The twelve apostles, left behind, crane their heads upwards to watch him go. Some of them, I think, are waving goodbye.

The interior of Saint-Sernin's basilica is a superb study in brick, beautifully harmonized, with twelve bays each 21 metres high set down the length of the church. Take binoculars to study the carvings at the top of the columns, some 500 altogether. In the present century long-concealed frescoes were discovered, dating from the thirteenth or early fourteenth century, depicting Christ in majesty. A romanesque crucifixion shows a Jesus whose face is almost blank, resigned to death.

The high altar of the consecration of 1096 is inscribed with the name of the man who carved it: Bernard Gilduin. Some have speculated that he also carved the seven fine figures in the passageway behind the high altar, one of which is a majestic Christ. Beardless, he has one hand raised in blessing, the other on a Bible inscribed '*Pax vobiscum*', and he is surrounded by the symbols of the four evangelists.

Under an eighteenth-century marble canopy is a relief sculpted by Marc Acis in 1720 depicting Saturninus's martyrdom.

But the chief glory of Saint-Sernin in the eyes of medieval pilgrims resided in none of these great works of art. Toulouse lay on a main pilgrimage route to Santiago de Compostela in Spain, where lay the body of St James the Great. *En route* pilgrims flocked to the basilica of Saint-Sernin for what they called 'the circuit of the holy bodies', relics of long-dead saints. Some of them lie in the chapels behind the high altar, but the greatest are in the crypt. The lower crypt houses pieces of five apostles – SS Philip, James the Less, James the Great, Simon and Jude. Said to have been donated to the church of Saint-Sernin by no less a personage than the Emperor Charlemagne himself, they are all in exquisite reliquaries.

Some of the many shrines depict the martyrdom of the saints whose relics are inside them. St Papoul, for instance, is beheaded, still wearing his bishop's mitre. Other shrines have towers modelled on that of the basilica itself. And here are two British saints: St Edmund the martyr, the only English king to be canonized, and St Gilbert of Sempringham, the only Englishman to found a medieval religious order.

Edmund, King of the East Angles, successfully resisted the Danish invaders until they defeated his army in 869. They tied him to a tree, scourged him, and, enraged by his continual prayers to Jesus, filled his body with arrows. Then they beheaded him. Edmund's followers reverently rescued his corpse and soon a cult grew around the dead king. A magnificent Benedictine abbey was founded at Bury St Edmunds in East Anglia, the monks praying for centuries around the saint's shrine.

How then did his remains and those of St Gilbert of Sempringham reach Toulouse? They were almost certainly stolen by the French prince Louis the Lion, when campaigning in England in 1216 against King John. Two years later Louis was besieging Toulouse, to whose great basilica he donated the holy bones.

Soon St Edmund was designated one of the eight protectors of the city. The canons of Saint-Sernin believed that he drove away the plague of 1631. In that year they opened his tomb to verify that all was well with the corpse, found it was in good order, and gave it a new silver reliquary. There it has remained to this day, coveted only by Cardinal Henry Vaughan at the beginning of this century, who wanted it for his new Catholic cathedral at Westminster in London, and today by the Anglican architect Stephen Dykes Bower, who would like it in the Anglican cathedral at Bury St Edmunds.

These relics, great though they be, are not the greatest in the basilica. In the upper crypt, in an eleventh-century reliquary made of Limoges enamel, you are shown a tiny piece of the cross on which Jesus was crucified. Here are St Remi's gloves and St Exupery's mitre. Here too, in a small silver shrine depicting his death (and angels receiving his soul into heaven), is all that remains on earth of St Saturninus – the most revered relic in the whole church. On this tiny base was constructed the greatest romanesque basilica in Europe.

Walk east of the basilica, looking back at its nine apsidal chapels, and along rue Saint-Bernard into the boulevard de Strasbourg which hosts a daily morning market selling fruit, vegetables, clothing and flowers. Boulevard de Strasbourg leads southeast into boulevard Lazare-Carnot, which in turn leads to the Toulouse war memorial and on the right one of the most lopsided cathedrals in Christendom.

Even before you go inside the cathedral you realize that its successive architects, working over seven centuries (from the eleventh to the seventeenth), quite simply failed to accept or complement what had been built before. In the west façade everything fights against and contradicts itself. Even the fine rose window is out of true with the graceful west doorway, which in turn is quite at odds with the massive brick keep of a bell-tower. The interior is even more

The thirteenth-century spire of Saint-Sernin, Toulouse, growing more elaborate as it rises above one of the city's shady streets.

disconcerting, with a romanesque nave crazily disjointed from the ogival choir.

On all but the west wall of this cathedral are exquisite chapels. One (on the right, dedicated to St Germaine) has macabre overtones. It contains the bodies of two cathedral canons, papal inquisitors who were killed at Avignonet in 1242, an act that provoked a bloody royal reprisal.

All these chapels repay examination – though to explore them all at once would give you something akin to indigestion. Look at one or two and then slip outside for a drink at one of the nearby cafés. One autumn I was sipping my wine here when a courteous Frenchman sat at the same table and, asking what I was drinking (a nondescript red wine, in fact), began an extremely instructive lecture on the vintages of the region. Toulouse, he said, was not at the centre of majestic vineyards, but the wines he personally laid down were certainly worth tasting. He bought them from a *domaine* at Fronton, not far north. As one might expect, he added, they were known as 'Côtes du Fronton'.

My new friend explained that the wines he bought from this merchant were mostly red. He knew exactly which slopes his wines came from – 'lots of what you would consider rubble, Monsieur, is precisely what gives these wines their special character', he announced. In addition the *vigneron* in question lets them ferment a long time. 'So' (my tutor moved into those strange wine-buffs' adjectives) 'I drink a lovely red – vigorous, even spicy, maybe a little woody as well.' He added that he also laid down a fruity demi-sec white from the same merchant, based on the Sémillon grape.

Then he made an astonishing offer. He lived, he said, just across the way. Would I like to see his cellar? My thirst buds wide awake, I instantly agreed. The cellar was remarkable: rows and rows of dusty bottles along with piles of old newspapers, discarded shoes and other rubbish. (What the French call a '*bazaar*'.)

Fiddling with his corkscrew my friend lightly stroked a bottle of what he described as the best of recent vintages. (It was 1978, I think.) And then, as I waited for him to open one, he made the craziest remark I have ever heard from a Frenchman: 'Monsieur, I would like to offer you a drink from one of these wines, but I cannot. You see, a wine has a memory, and this is the time of the wine harvest. All these wines are deeply unsettled and can't be touched just now.'

Such are the pleasures of taking a glass of wine near Toulouse cathedral. If you wish you can also picnic under the trees outside the cathedral where I once had a salutary encounter. I had selected my picnic lunch carefully – *paté*, salad bought in the local shops, some cheese, a bottle of sweet white wine. Next to me sat a native of the city, dressed in blue overalls, eating his own lunch. He began to talk to me. He himself was a builder; I said I was a writer. He offered me some of his powerfully-smelling sliced meats. I had no desire to give him any food of mine, but I weakly accepted. He offered me a glass of his own excellent red wine (I cannot say what it was, but he had it in a red plastic flask). Again I accepted, whereat he helped himself to most of my *paté*. As the vanquished do, I capitulated completely and offered him my wine too.

As an alternative to savouring the local hospitality, you can press on relentlessly to the splendidly restored Augustinian monastery. Begun in 1396, this has an elegant chapter house that was rebuilt in 1606 and is now a museum of religious art – with an outstanding collection of romanesque sculpture brought here from the older romanesque churches of Toulouse.

The route to the monastery/museum leads west along the rue Croix-Baragnon, a street adorned with fine ironwork like many in Toulouse. Don't miss the house at No. 15, half gothic, half romanesque, the oldest in Toulouse (for most others were burnt down in a fire of 1463). Then turn right along the rue des Arts with its half-timbered houses and sophisticated boutiques.

The museum displays many of its romanesque treasures in the ideal setting of its former monastic cloister, reserving the little cloister of 1626 for classical sculptures. From the cathedral has come a twelfth-century capital depicting King Herod lasciviously stroking Salome under the chin and a vivid carving of the beheading of John the Baptist, the executioner's sword half-way through the saint's neck, the saint's soul already being hugged by an angel. Another early twelfth-century carving shows two cross-legged women, one holding a little lion in her lap, the other carrying a ram. The museum's gothic masterpiece is a statue of Our Lady of Grace, dating from the mid sixteenth century, the virgin's face obedient, sublimely peaceful, a girl who has scarcely ceased to be a child.

If Toulouse is beginning to overwhelm you with its spiritual heritage, the rue du Languedoc running south from here brings you face to face with the secular splendour of the past. In the early sixteenth century the city became rich on woad, a dye made from a small plant flourishing in the area around. Merchants built themselves magical palaces, both sumptuous and ornate. Not to be outdone, members of the Toulouse parliament commissioned similarly fine houses.

That of the humanist Bishop of Rieux, Jean de Pins, is at No. 46 rue du Languedoc, while No. 36 is one of the most remarkable. Known as the Vieux Raisin (Old Grape) because it stood by an old inn, it was built for a merchant and lawyer named Bérenguier-Maynier in 1515 (and embellished thirty years later without spoiling its harmony). It stands behind an arcade, its abundantly decorated windows overlooking a shady courtyard. The Vieux Raisin is by the place des Carmes (named after a long-disappeared Carmelite monastery), whose ugly circular car-park covers a fine fish, fruit, chicken, *charcuterie* and honey market. This opens early in the morning, but tends to close at about lunchtime.

If you decided not to picnic by the cathedral, it is certainly time to take some refreshment now – perhaps in the nearby rue des Filatiers. Toulouse is a city of wide boulevards and vistas intermixed with intimate twisting medieval streets, and this is one of the latter, its open drain still running down the centre of the street. Opposite the tea and coffee restaurant is a four-storey half-timbered house built by a master goldsmith named Élie Gerauld in 1577 and now a baker's shop.

Next to it is one of many arcaded shops in this street, the arcade of stone, the three storeys of Toulouse brick.

Stone is rare in Toulouse. In 1606 a parliamentarian named François de Clary was living in a house designed by Nicolas Bachelier in 1538. He decided to add a rich baroque decoration in stone and caused a sensation. To this day his home is called the Stone House – *l'ostal de piera* in the tongue of the Languedoc. You reach it from the place des Carmes by walking west along the rue des Polinaires and turning left along the rue de la Dalbade. The Stone House is No. 25. Bachelier's courtyard is to my mind better than the baroque façade, decorated in a fashion Michelangelo would have approved of, with great swags and caryatids. One depicts an old man with a long beard, his hands folded in resignation as the centuries pass by.

Dalbade derives from *dea albata* and means 'white virgin', i.e. the mother of Jesus. Dominating this quarter is the church of Notre-Dame-de-la-Dalbade, built between 1505 and 1548, with six powerful buttresses each rising from a chapel. In the rue de la Dalbade itself is a magnificent stone doorway under a rose window, with a polychrome ceramic of the coronation of the Virgin Mary, a copy of Fra Angelico's original made in 1874 by the artist Gaston Virebent. The renaissance porch of 1537 is by Michel Colin, its statues (not the modern ones in the niches) by Hérigon Tailland.

Notre-Dame-de-la-Dalbade is surrounded by fine sixteenth- and seventeenth-century houses. Its tower was built by Nicolas Bachelier and is the highest in Toulouse (81 metres). This powerful symbol of the Church so much offended some eighteenth-century Revolutionaries that they tore it down. In 1881 it was rebuilt, only to fall down on the night of 11 April 1926, killing two bakers, Pascal Denax and his wife Anne. It also smashed the vault of the choir. Everything has been rebuilt and seems solid enough.

This part of the city is filled with fine houses. Abutting onto the church of the Dalbade is the former priory of the Knights of St John of Jerusalem, built by Jean-Pierre Rivalz in 1668 and now a school of

A stone head seeks inspiration on an arch of the city theatre, Toulouse.

commerce. The courtyard is lovely. (In this area of Toulouse, look at every courtyard you can enter and also every plaque.) Opposite is a house built in 1603. The Hôtel Molinier, No. 22 rue de la Dalbade, has a baroque doorway of 1556.

When the trade in indigo destroyed the market for woad (after the discovery of the route to India in 1560), Toulouse parliamentarians and *capitouls* supplanted the merchants as great builders. Walk back to the place des Carmes from the rue de la Dalbade along the rue Pharaon to admire some of their achievements, especially No. 47, the house of the *capitoul* Jean Marvejol, built in 1631. The design is complex, with a Louis XIII façade and richly decorated wooden galleries in the courtyard. No. 29 has a splendid Louis XVI façade. A relic of an earlier age is a tower of 1478

built by a bailiff named Noël Rolle. And these are but three of the ingredients of the rich architectural mixture in a single Toulouse street.

None of these buildings, despite their arrogance and splendour, can remotely compare to the brilliant Hôtel d'Assézat which Nicolas Bachelier designed for the woad merchant Pierre Assézat. Bachelier died before the work was completed, and the building was finished by Jean Castanié. It stands in the rue de Metz, reached from the Dalbade by taking the rue des Couteliers northwards.

Modelled on the Louvre and the palaces of Tuscany, the Hôtel d'Assézat achieves its own unique blend of baroque and renaissance fantasy. Doric, Ionic and Corinthian columns decorate the huge courtyard, with the two chief buildings joined together by a classical tower similar to those at Château Chambord in the Loire.

Today the Hôtel d'Assézat is the home of Europe's oldest literary society, the academy of the floral contests, founded in 1323 by seven citizens of Toulouse as the College du Gai Scavoir. They decided to sponsor a contest between poets on 3 May each year. The winner would be given a precious violet, shaped out of gold.

In 1324 the first winner was Arnaut Vidal, who gained his prize for a poem celebrating the Virgin Mary. Soon the success of the annual contests led others to offer prizes: jewelled eglantines, lilies, marigolds, primulas, carnations, amaranths, laurels. The most generous of these benefactors, the legendary Clémence Isaure, flourished in the fifteenth century. She is said to be represented in a funeral statue, carved in the fourteenth century, transformed into her likeness in the seventeenth and now in the Hôtel d'Assézat. In her hand is a bunch of these costly flowers.

Initially all the competing poets wrote in the language known as occitan – the *langue d'oc*. Until the ninth and tenth centuries the premier language of Gaul remained Latin, but a Latin that was slowly being modified. In the north of France it developed into the *langue d'oïl*, basically present-day French. But in the south the people spoke one of five dialects, all collectively described as the *langue d'oc*.

This was the language of the troubadours, who enriched it with songs of courtly love and knightly valour. Among their number, alongside beggars and wandering minstrels, were Arnaut Daniel whom Dante dubbed the prince of poetry, and the churchman Gui Folqueis, who became Pope Clement IV. Others, such as Peire Vidal, son of a Toulouse fur merchant, travelled as far as Arabia, singing the praises of love.

The *langue d'oïl* triumphed over the *langue d'oc* with the crusade against the Albigensian heresy and the ascension of the seigneurs of northern France. For a brief moment in the late sixteenth and early seventeenth century there was a resurgence of a baroque occitan. Pierre Goudelin of Toulouse published his *Ramelet moundi*, the first ever collection of occitan poetry. But the centralization of the reign of Louis XIV, when all power was securely based on Paris, stifled the movement. In 1694 the College du Gai Scavoir at Toulouse was transformed by royal behest into the Academy of Floral Games.

Only in the nineteenth century did the people of the Languedoc again begin to savour the beauty of their traditional tongue. In 1854, inspired by the poet Frédéric Mistral, who believed that poetry transformed humans into gods, a movement called the 'Félibrige' was begun, its avowed aim 'to preserve for ever the occitan nation, its language, traditions, way of life and all that constitutes its spirit'. Significantly, their symbol was a golden rod with seven branches, symbolizing the seven men of 1323 who founded the College du Gai Scavoir at Toulouse.

Against all odds the Félibrige movement triumphed. Literary giants like Lamartine, Alfred de Vigny, Villiers de l'Isle-Adam, Theophil Gautier and Mallarmé enthused over the *langue d'oc*, even though not one of them spoke a word of it. Since 1951 the *langue d'oc* has been taught at the Academy of Toulouse, with 10,000 students a year registering for courses in it.

Oddly enough Lamartine had failed to win even the lowliest prize when he competed in the Toulouse Floral Games of 1818. The following year Victor Hugo

The profitable woad trade enriched the merchants of early sixteenth-century Toulouse, enabling them to build sumptuous town houses, invariably with splendid renaissance doorways.

triumphed. His poem was an ode on the restoration of the statue of King Henri IV to the new bridge.

The *pont neuf* is in fact not the newest but the oldest bridge in Toulouse. It spans the river a few metres west of the Hôtel d'Assézat, past the former monastic church of the Daurade whose present eighteenth-century building replaced a gallo-roman church destroyed in 1761. Nicolas Bachelier designed the bridge in 1544. Building its seven graceful arches took another 128 years, with the help of two other master architects, Pierre Souffron and Jacques Lemercier (the Parisian who designed the church of the Sorbonne).

Across the river are the seventeenth-century hospital of Saint-Jacques (whose foundation dates from 1275) and, upstream, the dome of the hospice of Saint-Joseph-de-la-Grave. This classical dome is

Above The classical dome of the hospice of Saint-Joseph-de-la-Grave, seen across the River Garonne, inspired the novelist Stendhal to declare that Toulouse was the Rome of the Languedoc.

Right The elegant early fourteenth-century cloisters of the former Jacobin monastery at Toulouse offer a moment of peace in a lively city.

presumably what prompted the early nineteenth-century novelist Stendhal to make the surprising observation that this romanesque and medieval city reminded him of Rome. Walk north from the *pont neuf* (along the quai de la Daurade and the place de la Daurade) to be plunged into medieval Toulouse at its most breathtaking.

In 1215, at the pope's request, St Dominic founded an order of preachers in Toulouse in order to combat the Cathar heresy. Here they began building a church and cloister, finishing the work only in the fourteenth century. They added a bell-tower 45 metres high which echoed the bell-tower of Saint-Sernin.

A former monk who became Bishop of Pamiers paid for the building of the chapel of Saint-Antonin in 1339. Antonin was the patron saint of his diocese and superb frescoes depict scenes from his life and the visions of St John the Divine. Almost certainly the bishop brought wall painters for this work from the papal court at Avignon. Pope Urban V considered the whole building so superb that in 1369 he commanded that the body of St Thomas Aquinas be transferred here from Italy.

This convent, known as the monastery of the Jacobins, became a cavalry barracks under Napoleon Bonaparte and remained such until 1864. The windows were bricked up; horses were shod in the sacristy; the chapel of Saint-Antonin became a hospital for sick animals. The building has been magnificently re-stored. No stay in Toulouse, however short, should exclude a visit to the monastery, if only to marvel at the two parallel brick naves of the church, separated by stone columns – from the seventh of which rise twenty-two groins resembling a huge palm tree.

West of the church of the Jacobins is the place Saint-Pierre (whose church of Saint-Pierre-des-Cuisines, dating from the eleventh and fifteenth centuries, boasts romanesque capitals illustrating the lives of SS Peter and Paul and a romanesque doorway). The quays and tree-lined canals of this part of Toulouse give it a quiet charm, with barges still sailing through the city. The quai Saint-Pierre leads from here alongside the Garonne to the canal which Loménie de Brienne created in 1770. After a half-hour's walk the canal runs into the basin of the Pont-Jumeaux, where the Garonne meets the great Canal du Midi. Here a delightful bas-relief sculpted by François Lucas in 1775 depicts the province of Languedoc entreating the water goddess to link the great river with the Mediterranean.

Leave Toulouse northeast by the avenue de Lyon and the rue du Faubourg-Bonnefoy to drive along the N88 towards Gaillac. The road leaves the *département* of Haute-Garonne and enters that of the Tarn, passing villages that appear peaceful today but still give a hint of past savagery.

Saint-Sulpice-la-Pointe, for instance, reached after 29 kilometres (watch for the signs on the right), is based on a fortified town founded by Sicard d'Alaman in 1247. Decimated by the plague in the fourteenth and sixteenth centuries and sacked by the Huguenots in 1562, Saint-Sulpice retains vestiges of its old château, as well as a church with an enormous bell-tower gable – the largest in the whole *département*. Once its pride was a fourteenth-century ivory triptych, but when the nave fell down in 1884 the State rebuilt the church only on condition that it could transport the triptych to the Cluny museum near Mâcon.

One of the proselytes of Languedoc culture, Edmond Cabet, was born here in 1846 (he died in 1909), and a plaque to the right of the town hall marks his birthplace. Follow the N88 alongside the River Tarn for another 3 kilometres to reach Rabastens, birthplace of one of the poets Cabet celebrated: the Huguenot Augier Gaillard, who was also a soldier and who was known as Lou Roudié de Rabastens in the Languedoc tongue. On his statue, which shows him wearing a sixteenth-century bowler hat, he is described as 'either the last Languedoc troubadour or the first poet of his *patois*', an inscription that perfectly illustrates the decline of a once noble language to the lowly status of a dialect. Nevertheless, the inscription continues, Gaillard's rustic muse was honoured by Kings Charles IX, Henri III and Henri IV.

The massive fortified bell-tower of the church of Notre-Dame-du-Bourg at Rabastens (topped with two rather puny six-sided pepperpots with pointed hats) lours at a potentially hostile world with the same curmudgeonliness as that at Saint-Sulpice, but the interior of the church is quite different in atmosphere. Once your eyes become accustomed to the gloom, splendid wall paintings appear, some of them dating from as far back as the thirteenth century. The church also has an unspoilt romanesque doorway. The profitable woad trade enabled the citizens of Rabastens to build the first major gothic nave in the Tarn, inspired by the Jacobin church at Toulouse, as well as the charming half-timbered houses. These shelter behind the ramparts as if fearful that de Montfort might return (he attacked Rabastens in 1211 and took it in 1212), or that one day the town might relive the savagery of the Wars of Religion.

A warmer thought is that grapes have been grown here since the thirteenth century. Rabastens today has a co-operative of 550 wine merchants cultivating 1515 hectares of vines between them, which produce around 100,000 hectolitres of wine, nearly all of it red.

The route to Gaillac runs through maize fields, trees and sunflowers as well as vineyards, passing Lisle-sur-Tarn on the way. This small town is well worth a visit for a trip on the river, for its arcades, its over-hanging houses, its tree-lined market square with a fountain and its church, whose thirteenth-century tower has a doorway proclaiming in Latin 'This is the house of God and the gate of Heaven'.

Gaillac itself, 25 kilometres from Saint-Sulpice, often seems to me totally tumbledown, but for an indescribably charming experience. Walk to the bridge over the Tarn where the ancient abbey church of Saint-Michel scarcely avoids falling into the river. The romanesque east end is in good order; a seventeenth-century statue of Our Lady in her Sorrows is worth seeking out; the high altar is eighteenth-century baroque; and the organ is by a native of this region who was one of the finest organ builders in France (and one of the most prolific), Cavaillé-Coll.

The town was founded by the Benedictines in the early tenth century, reaching its apogée, architecturally speaking, in the thirteenth. And yet under-neath its sleepiness it is still healthy. Its sleepiness, I think, is really an outward manifestation of Gaillac's peaceable nature in a region that has seen much savagery. One of the most celebrated monks of the abbey of Saint-Michel was Dom Vaisette, who was born in the year Louis XIV decided to revoke toleration for Protestants (1685) and died in 1756. He wrote a five-volume history of Languedoc, but stopped at the year 1643, 'fearing', as he said 'that he would not find himself able to speak of his contemporaries with sufficient candour'. And his history was astonishingly kind to the Huguenots and heretics who might, one would have thought, have been his chief enemies, for Dom Vaisette considered that he and they were languedociens first and foremost.

Another distinguished son of Gaillac was the pioneering anatomist and surgeon Antoine Portal. In spite of having been ennobled by the last king of the ancien régime, Louis XVI, Antoine's universally recognized merits spared him from harm at the hands of the Revolutionaries, and he continued to work happily till his death in 1832 at the age of ninety.

The most warlike son of Gaillac in modern times is commemorated in a statue in the main square. Jean-Joseph d'Hautpoul was born in a nearby hamlet in 1754 and became one of Napoleon's generals. He fought nobly at Hohenlinden and Austerlitz and on 8 February 1807 was mortally wounded at the battle of Eylau. Napoleon himself decreed that twenty-four cannons taken at Eylau should be melted down to make an equestrian statue of d'Hautpoul, dressed in his curassier's uniform.

Each May Gaillac hosts a festival of music; I have caught dazzling trumpet and organ concerts in its old abbey. And the famous wine fair starts on the first Thursday in August, with fireworks, equestrian tours of the vineyards, prize-givings and, of course, tastings. The red- and black-robed knights of the order of the 'Dive Bouteille de Gaillac' (known in langue d'oc as the ancient 'Compagnha del Rey de Poda') solemnly taste each year's vintages, and present the accolades to those they judge to be the finest wines of the year. All of them have sworn 'to love and defend both vine and wine, children of the sun and the patience of mankind . . . and to live in peace, joy and health'.

Just opposite the abbey church I once took a drink with the moustachioed artist who draws the seductive covers for the catalogue of the wine fair (some such picture as a couple in local costume, the blonde on the peasant's knee, she waving a glass). Inside his studio sketches wittily illustrate different sorts of wine: a clapped out old car stands for wine that somehow hasn't balanced its acidity, tannin and maturity. A wine that slips too easily down the throat is depicted through a Burlington Bertie figure, tipsily sitting in the road, his top hat floating away.

Gaillac wines are older than the town itself, since the Romans planted vines here. Naturally the Benedictine monks sternly regulated their quality. In the twelfth and thirteenth century the English began importing them and today the vineyards spread northwards as far as Cordes. Some of the wines are slightly sparkling: *appellation blanc perlé; mousseux brut méthode gaillacoise; mousseux doux méthode gaillacoise*. Others are powerful reds, especially those grown on the gravelly left bank of the Tarn. The right bank is more sheltered, its red wines subtler, its whites fruity. The red wines derive their tang chiefly from a grape known as Duras, with the powerful Servadou adding richness and some Braucol adding tannin. The whites are mostly based on the Mauzac grape (and to my mind their colour is as much golden as white). Gamay varieties produce a pleasing rosé Gaillac.

People here will tell you to drink the sparkling wines immediately, the whites and rosés young, and the reds when you want to. They drink the *vins mousseux* very cold, with pâtisserie and cheese and fruit. They drink the *vins blancs perlés* as an aperitif or with the hors d'oeuvre. The young reds they will drink preferably at about 10°C; the older ones as warm as 12°, or even 14°. And for perking up the spirits I like nothing more than the sparkling white *Pétillant de Raisin*.

Once I took my niece Elizabeth to Gaillac. We both ate *cassoulet*. Elizabeth asked me if I would mind trying hers. Hers, like mine, seemed to me to have been made out of terrifyingly old beans, wrapped up in pigskin. That day I was glad to clear my throat with the roughest, wildest red Gaillac.

Gaillac is an excellent spot to begin a tour of the splendid Tarn bastides, a word which connotes a new town in the *langue d'oc*. They were developed (sometimes on the site of older towns) after 1271 when the French monarchy inherited the possessions of the counts of Toulouse. More than 300 were founded in the Languedoc, as the inhabitants of the region looked forward to an era of new prosperity.

The plans of these bastides almost invariably included streets bisecting each other at right angles and an arcaded market square. Their citizens often secured the right to elect councillors, the privilege of self-government and exemption from military service. In the earlier bastides Cathars often hoped to live unmolested by the orthodox. As a result of the troubled times of the Albigensian crusade and English raids during the Hundred Years War, the inhabitants usually decided that no bastide was complete without powerful and sometimes highly ingenious fortifications.

To tour the major bastides of the Tarn, take the D922 north for 5 kilometres or so from Gaillac to where it meets the D964 and here turn left for the hilltop town of Castelnau-de-Montmiral. Castelnau-de-Montmiral was in fact founded in the first quarter of the thirteenth century by Raymond VII of Toulouse and passed into the hands of Arnaud de Trian, the nephew of Pope John XXII, at the beginning of the next century. The remains of the fourteenth-century fortifications (which were destroyed at the beginning of the seventeenth century), along with the ancient town gate, are still there, as well as several more or less ruined châteaux. Its site is splendid: 'Montmiral' means 'admirable' or 'delightful' hill. Its fifteenth-century gothic church displays a sliver of the True

---

East of Toulouse the industrial town of Mazamet is set amidst hills and ravines, with splendid walking country where commerce is speedily forgotten.

Cross, decorated with 210 of its sometime 350 precious stones.

Continue westwards along the D964 until the D8 runs right to take you up to Puycelci after some 9 kilometres. At a bend in the road half way up artists sit drawing and painting the threatening, grey, formidable walls of this Cathar town that Simon de Montfort took in 1211 and that resisted the English throughout the fourteenth century. Walk up to the fifteenth-century church of Saint-Corneille with its imposing tower (you can make out the date 1777 on the tower) – a fine venue for frequent concerts in summer. On the north side of the church, through the two arches of the tower, are seats under shady acacia and chestnut trees, and a half-timbered house with a sunken lower floor and steps to the first storey. Another church, built by the villagers in honour of St Roch after he had performed his traditional function of delivering them from the plague, now serves as the local tourist office.

Puycelci is a village of narrow streets and overhanging roofs, with incredible views of the surrounding countryside: the rich valley of the River Vère, vineyards and terraces, and to the north the 3500 hectares of the Grésigne forest. Although the predominant red oaks, Douglas firs, pines and chestnuts of this forest were planted comparatively recently, the forest itself is ancient. The King of France bought it from the Count of Toulouse in the thirteenth century. Until the nineteenth century it was profitably exploited by the villagers of Puycelci, who used the wood to make staves for barrels, which they then transported in bulk to the coopers of Gaillac. Charcoal burners from as far away as the Vosges and the Auvergne migrated here. That whole economy is no more. But the forest still shelters about forty stags, two hundred deer and a hundred or so wild boars.

Alongside the D964 northwest of Puycelci the ruins of the château at Bruniquel perch on a rock 100 metres above the River Aveyron. A graceful renaissance wing, still intact, sets off the sterner gothic fortress dating from the eleventh and twelfth centuries. Its name allegedly derives from its sixth-century foundress, Brunhehaut, daughter of a Visigoth king. Its views are superb. And 5 kilometres northeast the fortified village of Penne contains what Freda White described in her *Three Rivers of France* as the strangest of all the châteaux of the Tarn, a castle 'so improbable that you do not believe in it even as you look at it'.

Standing on the narrow isthmus of a promontory between the right bank of the Aveyron and the ravine known in the *langue d'oc* as Cap de Biaou (which means bull's head), the thirteenth- and fourteenth-century buildings of the château at Penne seem to defy the laws of gravity, crazily overhanging the great limestone rock. As if this were not fantastic enough, Penne also boasts a prehistoric cave, the grotte de la Madeleine, in which late Stone Age artists sculpted remarkable wall reliefs, including a massive reclining lady known as the Venus of Penne.

The D174 and D115 now wind precariously alongside the Aveyron gorge by way of the exquisite medieval town of Saint-Antonin-Noble-Val, whose town hall is an extremely rare twelfth-century secular building and whose ancient houses include the delightfully named Maison de l'Amour. The road continues east alongside the river by way of Varen, another medieval village with half-timbered houses, as far as Laguépie, where the Aveyron meets the Viaur. In pursuit of Cathars, Simon de Montfort sacked the town in 1212.

Laguépie lies 13 kilometres north of the most outstanding of all the bastides of the Tarn, Cordes, whose houses swarm to the top of a peak 70 metres high, justifying its full title, Cordes-sur-Ciel (Cordes in the sky). Count Raymond VII of Toulouse founded Cordes in 1222 to administer one of his vast estates. The foundation charter, dated 14 November 1222, still exists. From the beginning Cordes was defended not by one powerful set of defensive walls but by two, each of which still retains a couple of gates.

The bastide brought stability and peace to the region. Linen and hemp were grown in the surrounding countryside. Although the area was ravaged by the Black Death in 1350, wealthy merchants, leather workers, dyers and weavers continued to prosper here until the end of the fourteenth century, building a quite exceptional collection of rich gothic houses. Cordes welcomed many Cathar heretics in the fourteenth century, but wisely declined to provoke the Inquisition, and in 1321 the town consuls publicly apologized on behalf of the people for any deviance from orthodoxy.

The town is bisected east-west by the steep Grand'rue, which you enter from the west by way of the powerful porte de la Jane, flanked by a couple of semicircular towers. A remnant of old Cordes is the curious cobbler's sign carved over the lintel of a door on the left just after you pass through the gate. Today Cordes is the home of painters, weavers and jewellery makers with a shrewd eye for the tourist trade – though without these men and women, inspired chiefly by the painter Yves Brayer, who came here in 1940, Cordes would never have been restored to its present beautiful self.

Almost immediately you come to the most fortified of the four town entrances, the porte des Ormeaux, again with two great towers, and once boasting a portcullis and a massive wooden door. Take the left fork and climb up to the church of Saint-Michel, with an apse dating from the thirteenth century, a belfry dating from the next century, and an organ which came from Notre-Dame-de-Paris in 1840. The modern decoration of the walls and vault was painted by Yves Brayer. The belfry is connected to a watch tower, the highest point of the bastide – an entirely practical arrangement since the look-out would ring the church bell to warn of an approaching danger.

Further up the street to the right is the very centre of the bastide, the covered market place, whose monumental roof is supported by twenty-four octagonal stone pillars. On the south side is the medieval town well, an astonishing 114 metres deep. A plaque records that the nearby iron cross commemorates three inquisitors, sent to Cordes in search of Cathars by the Bishop of Albi and thrown down the well. Apart from the fact that the citizens would hardly have thus poisoned their drinking water, the legend is not supported by a single historical document.

Go through the market square into the Grand'rue and you will see the elegant house of the falconer (Maison du grand Fauconnier) on your left, one of the finest of the medieval buildings of Cordes (and well restored by Viollet-le-Duc in the nineteenth century). Its name derives from the carved birds that once decorated its façade. Inside the courtyard a fifteenth-century staircase leads to a museum of the work of Cordes' most celebrated artist, Yves Brayer. Next to it is the rose-grey Maison Prunet, beautifully restored after a fire by the sculptor Jean-Marc, who came to Cordes in 1958. And further down the Grand'rue on the way back to the west gates you reach first the Maison Fontpeyrouse (with its lovely courtyard and two storeys of wooden galleries) and then one of the oldest buildings in the bastide, the Maison du grand Veneur. 'Veneur' means hunter, and the house is marvellously decorated with a frieze of sculpted animals and huntsmen over the graceful gothic windows of its third floor. In the very centre of the frieze is a strange carving of the head of a man and his wife, taken by some to be Count Raymond VII and his spouse.

The fifth of Cordes' finest buildings is the house of the horseman (Maison du grand Écuyer). Now a hotel, it derives its name from the horse's head that juts out like a gargoyle from one corner (though it could equally well have been called after the carved lady who chews an apple, or the man playing bagpipes, or after one of the fantastic beasts carved on the façade).

These are not the only delights of Cordes. The *barbacane*, a huge tower set in the ramparts at the east end of the town near the porte de l'Horloge, is well worth seeking out. And the steps leading down to the porte du Planol from this gateway, whose clock is set under a jolly pepperpot tower, are exceedingly romantic – though not recommended for those with weary legs. (The steep steps are known as the 'Pater Noster', since they are as numerous as the words in the Lord's Prayer.)

If Cordes is stupendous, so is Albi 25 kilometres southeast. From Albi derives the word Albigensian, the English name for the heresy properly known as

Catharism. Cathars in fact spread far beyond Albi. In 1163 Pope Alexander III told a council at Tours that the heresy had started around Toulouse and then spread like a cancer into Gascony and elsewhere.

The pope was right about the spread of the heresy and wrong about its origin. Undoubtedly the Cathars derived some of their beliefs from the Persians and the Zoroastrian division of the world into the principles of good and evil, a dualism dominated by God and by Satan. For Cathars, the material world lay in the realm of the latter.

The word 'Cathar' derives from a Greek word meaning 'pure', and the leaders of the movement, who called themselves the perfect ones, rejected even marriage as partaking of Satan's realm. Inevitably they abhorred the sacraments of the Church, since these involved material elements like bread, wine and water. They also rejected any food which was the product of sexual breeding.

Their humbler followers were often less austere and postponed the *consolamentum* until the end of their lives. This was the Cathar equivalent of baptism, which gained them entry, so they believed, to the Kingdom of Heaven. In consequence a good number of them managed to live carnal enough lives with a decent conscience. They are even said to have invented one of the delicacies of this region, *la navette albigeoise* – a cake made from crushed almonds perfumed with orange blossom.

At the beginning of the thirteenth century Pope Innocent III initially hoped to convert the Cathars simply by sending them Catholic preachers. In 1208, however, one of his legates was assassinated by an officer of Count Raymond VI of Toulouse, who was known to be favourable to Catharism. When the news reached the pope, he remained silent for two days. Then he called for a crusade against the heretics.

The massive, menacing cathedral of Saint-Cecilia, Albi, seen across the River Tarn.

Simon de Montfort's savagery in the crusade was matched by that of other leaders. The city of Béziers was taken in 1209 and its whole Cathar population – something like 20,000 persons – massacred. Cathar cities like Minerve and Lavaur were pillaged and ravaged. In 1228 Raymond VII of Toulouse expiated his father's error by submitting to St Louis, King of France. He was publicly whipped, a mild penalty compared with most. The last refuge of the heretics, the château at Montségur, was taken only after an eight months siege in 1244. Two hundred of its defenders, along with their families, were burnt alive.

The heresy lingered on. When Bernard de Castanet became Bishop of Albi in 1276 he continued to persecute suspected Cathars. In 1300 thirty-five nobles were put on trial in Albi. Nineteen of them were found guilty of Cathar beliefs and practices and shackled for the rest of their lives. Heretics even reappeared at Béziers in the early fourteenth century.

Meanwhile the new cathedral had been founded by Bernard de Castanet in 1282. Since one of his predecessors had been virtually imprisoned in the old cathedral by the heretics, the new one was built like a vast fortress. As you drive down into the city from Cordes, the houses appear as a beautiful pink array. Then you reach the river, the oldest of whose three bridges dates from 1306, and the huge rose-red brick cathedral dominates everything, its nave alone 90 metres long, 28 metres wide, and 30 metres high.

The cathedral was built over two centuries, delayed in part by the depredations of the English during the Hundred Years War. Outside it remains basically romanesque, with some fine delicate gothic decorations on the two upper storeys of its massive tower. A startling exception to this stern fortress-like exterior is the fifteenth-century entrance on the south side, covered by a highly decorated porch built out of white stone in the sixteenth century.

In extraordinary contrast to the sombre exterior, there are the most entrancing decorations imaginable inside the church. At the west end, beneath the organ case built by Christophe Moucherel in 1737, is a late fifteenth-century fresco of the Last Judgment. The left-hand scene, the resurrection of the just, is splendidly symbolic: beneath the angels and the twelve apostles sit illustrious French Christians, including Charlemagne, St Louis and Blanche de Castile. Beneath them the naked dead, risen from their graves, walk delicately along with the books of their lives open on their chests. Below them the unfortunates are dragged down by demons. Reading from the left these damned are respectively the proud, the envious, the angry and (crossing over to the right-hand scene) the miserly, the greedy and the self-indulgent.

Yet more remarkable are the extravagant stone choir screen and another richly carved screen which encloses the whole choir. Once the niches of the choir screen were filled with statues of saints, but the Revolutionaries destroyed these as superstitious. Adam and Eve survive, covering their nakedness not with fig-tree leaves (as the Bible has it), but with vines (as any son or daughter of Albi might do).

Polychrome statues of the Virgin Mary, the apostles and the Old Testament prophets still embellish the screen around the choir, along with exquisite representations of the Old Testament heroines Judith and Esther. Amongst the prophets the statue of Jeremiah is certainly the finest, while the Christian saints include a lovely statue of St Cecilia, to whom Albi cathedral is dedicated. To crown the whole, at the beginning of the sixteenth century Italian artists from Lombardy and Emilia decorated the vault of the cathedral with more prophets, saints and the story of Jesus.

Langue d'oc for bishop is *besbié*, and the bishop's palace, the palais de la Berbie, stands on the edge of the Tarn north of the cathedral. Its fine gardens overlook the old bridge. Across the river pink brick houses grow on the wall that rises from the water's edge. Long disused steps climb down to boats that have disappeared. The palace itself, fortified like the church, was built between the thirteenth and fifteenth centuries and today houses more than 600 works of art by the tragic crippled genius Henri de Toulouse-Lautrec.

The bold Italianate swags and lions over the entrance to the theatre at Castres, designed by the architect Joseph Galinier in 1904.

Toulouse-Lautrec was born at Albi in 1864 in the Hôtel du Bosc (in the rue de l'École-Mage, and open to visitors), to a well-off family descended from the counts of Toulouse. 'Henri chirps like a cricket from morning to night, brightening up the whole house,' wrote his grandmother. In 1878, at the age of fourteen, he fell from a chair and broke his thigh bone. Scarcely was the fracture healed when he fell again and broke his thigh bone a second time. It appears that Toulouse-Lautrec suffered from a deficiency which left his bones unusually brittle. After these accidents his legs never developed properly, so that although the rest of his body grew, by the time he was an adult his stunted legs meant he stood only 1½ metres tall. His remedy for low spirits during his short life (he died in 1901) was art.

The palais de la Berbie is a gallery to visit and revisit. Here are Toulouse-Lautrec's early sketches of his parents, as well as Toulouse-Lautrec himself painted by Édouard Vuillard. Another drawing (done in 1889 by Louis Anquetin) shows the poor wasted legs. Here are the famous posters: Jane Avril dancing at the Moulin Rouge, her career launched by Toulouse-Lautrec himself who had come across her working as a chorus girl; Louise Weber, the blonde known as La Goulue (the glutton), who would kick off her partner's hat dancing at the Moulin de la Galette; the delightful Yvette Guilbert, caricatured in her long black gloves.

Here too are some of the masterpieces he painted in Parisian houses of ill-fame, the best of all to my mind undoubtedly the scene of sad-faced girls sitting in the salon of the rue des Moulins in 1894. Here are his crayon sketches of circuses, and more restful paintings: his cousin Marie Dilhau playing the piano; another cousin (and inseparable companion), the pensive Dr Taplé de Céleyran, at the Comédie Française in 1894; his friend the Parisian dressmaker Renée Vert.

Old Albi is a city of delightful narrow streets with timber-framed overhanging houses, towers and staircases. Its church of Saint-Salvi boasts a cool eleventh-century cloister. In the pâtisseries look out for the triangular biscuits known as *les petits Janots*, called after a chef named Janot who first thought to mix a few grains of aniseed with the paste. Or try the *gimblettes*, a biscuit piquantly flavoured with citron.

The N112 runs for 40 kilometres south from Albi to Castres. About half-way is the bastide of Réalmont, which Guillaume de Cohardon, seneschal of Carcassonne, founded in 1272 on behalf of his lord Philippe the Bold, King of France. Its fortifications were razed after the town turned Protestant and was reconquered for the Catholics by the Prince de Condé in 1628. Today a lively market each Wednesday is devoted to the pink garlic and succulent fowl of the region.

Castres is even older, its name deriving from a fortified Roman camp (*castrum*) close by which Charlemagne founded a Benedictine monastery in 810. From the north you drive in past the magnificent gardens and fountain, designed by Le Nôtre in 1676. The seventeenth-century baroque cathedral dedicated to St Benedict still retains its romanesque tower. Opposite is the town hall, once the bishop's palace, and built by J. H. Mansart between 1666 and 1669. Today it houses the finest museum of Spanish art in France, its greatest treasures the nightmarish visions of Goya: men carrying donkeys, witches on broomsticks, a priest in his vestments walking a tightrope.

From here walk along the banks of the River Agout to the place Jean-Jaurès. On the opposite bank tall medieval houses overhang the river, built in stone and wood by tanners and weavers, their cellars opening out into the water. In the *place* brightly-coloured canopies cover the market stalls on Saturday and Tuesday mornings. Gabriel Pech set up a statue in 1924 here to the most famous son of Castres in modern times, the fiery socialist Jean Jaurès, who was born in 1859 and assassinated in Paris on 31 July 1914. Close by I have drunk rich fish soup and eaten *les nougatines castraises*, a sugary nougat of almonds and crushed hazel-nuts.

Even as you drive into Castres, the ridges of the granite massif known as the Sidobre come into view. To explore this extraordinary region drive east to La Fontasse. Just to the south of the town is a river of granite rocks, the 'chaos de la Roquette', left by a stream which goes underground just before it reaches the debris.

Turn northwest to Burlats, a village dominated by the massive 'rock of Paradise'. At first the whole of Burlats seems to be a sad deplorable ruin, but it is still worth exploring, if only to conjure up its rich, tragic history in your imagination. Here around the year 850 the followers of St Benedict of Aniane founded a priory. Here in 1155 was born the beautiful granddaughter of Louis VI, Adelaide, who married Count Roger II of Trencavel, the protector of the Cathars, at the age of sixteen. Widowed in 1194, she

created a glittering court at Burlats, patronizing such troubadours as Arnaud de Mareuil.

Burlats prospered until the Wars of Religion. Then the Protestants sacked the little town in 1573. The monks fled to Castres. After the death of Henri IV religious bitterness flared up again. In 1622 soldiers of the Protestant Duke de Rohan set fire to the church. In 1628 the whole village was sacked by Condé's vengeful soldiers. Three years later Richelieu ordered the demolition of Burlat's fortifications. Today only two towers remain.

None the less I find it amazing that the church has been left open to the elements ever since the monks departed for Castres over two and a half centuries ago. The town hall and a little local school occupy a partly rebuilt north side; on the south side, where three stone seats for the priests once were, is a row of toilets. Round the back is a crucifixion group restored in 1937 as a thank-offering for the Christian mission of that year – which evidently failed, if the number of worshippers I saw at Mass in the new church of Saint-Pierre is anything to go by!

Cross the river and take the D4 left to Roquecourbe. The route is lovely, the town with its arcades picturesque. From here the D30 runs east to Lacrouzette, through part of the Sidobre that was inhabited in prehistoric times, and to the most remarkable sight of the region, the balanced granite mass known as Peyro Clabado ('pinned rock'). From the centre of Lacrouzette near the hotel climb the rue du Sidobre and follow the signposts to this extraordinary rock. Weighing 780 tonnes, it is balanced precariously on a much smaller rock with a base that can be scarcely a square metre in area.

Etymologists think the word Sidobre derives from the Latin *sine opere*, 'without work' or 'without cultivation', and that this in turn reflects the barren ruggedness of the terrain. Today there is work here. Profitable quarries abound, some of them close by Peyro Clabado, with skilled craftsmen working pink,

The bizarre granite rock known as Peyro Clabado. Note the little pebbles left on top by bachelors seeking good luck in courtship.

grey and white granite. Around 1200 quarrymen hew some 100,000 tonnes of Sidobre granite a year. Near Peyro Clabado you can picnic on granite seats and tables. Close by is a granite cabin which once – and only once – served me *crêpes* and coffee with (of all things) powdered milk.

Peyro Clabado is but one of many bizarre granite formations in the Sidobre. Some huge boulders are so precariously balanced as to rock. Others have been given names, such as the three cheeses (which balance one on top of the other like three granite chunks of *chèvre*) and the goose. Both are close by Peyro Clabado. (Look for the signposts to Le Roc de l'Oie – the rock of the goose – as you leave.)

Not surprisingly legends abound about the giants or

Market day at Castres stirs the taste buds.

The memory of the dead of the French Resistance is still treasured, as here in the Sidobre.

supernatural powers who created these fantastic rock structures. Some have been ascribed to petrified elephants or huge petrified birds. The formations themselves have been endowed with various remarkable powers. The pile of little stones on top of Peyro Clabado, for instance, has been placed there by generations of bachelors competing against each other in the belief that the first one to climb to the top and set his pebble there will be sure to marry the girl of his desire within a year.

The natural explanation of these enigmatic rock formations seems to me no less fascinating than the legendary ones. At first sight granite seems harder, more homogeneous than most other natural rocks. In truth the granite of the Sidobre is fissured, and over

the centuries the weaker areas have partly decomposed into sand, leaving behind only the hardest rock, often in these strangely twisted forms.

The road from Peyro Clabado (D58) winds through the Sidobre past the rock of the three cheeses and with fine prospects of the gorge of the Agout. Where it joins the D53, turn right to Ferrières.

This little town was a Calvinist stronghold throughout the sixteenth century. Its leading Protestant seigneur, Guillaume de Guilhot, died in 1575 as governor of Castres, having implacably attacked Catholics whilst at the same time patronizing the most exquisite renaissance artists. He restored the eleventh-century château of Ferrières, which ironically became the home of a garrison pledged to hunt down Protestants hiding in the mountains after Louis XIV decided to end religious toleration in France. Today part of the château at Ferrières houses the most important Protestant museum in the upper Languedoc.

The D53 winds southeast by the river from here to Brassac, a large village of white stone houses with blue roofs, with a lovely, very early gothic bridge that has spanned the river since 1193.

The river at this point separates the territory of the seigneurs of Belfortès (on the left bank) from that of the seigneurs of Castelnau (on the right bank). In consequence Brassac boasts two châteaux, one for each lord, each warning the other not to venture too far outside his own property. That of Belfortès, now a hotel, still preserves its thirteenth-century tower. The château of Castelnau was besieged in 1569 by Protestant troops commanded by Gontaud de Biron, who put its twenty Catholic defenders to death. He would have spared the châtelaine, who was hiding in bed surrounded by her daughters; but a Protestant soldier whose own family had been grievously treated by Catholics put a pistol to her head and blew it away.

Since 1193 this old bridge has crossed the River Agout at Brassac. It leads to the château taken in 1569 by the Huguenots, who proceeded to massacre their Catholic opponents.

Follow the D622 back east to Castres, and continue west along the D112 for 39 kilometres to Lavaur. If Brassac is redolent with the savagery of the Wars of Religion, Lavaur reminds you of earlier religious viciousness, for when Simon de Montfort took it from the Cathars after a two months siege in 1211, he massacred the defenders and flung the heretical châtelaine, Dame Guiraude, weeping and screaming, into the town well. Her brother, Sire Aimery, and eighty other Cathars were hanged like common thieves. The site of her château makes a pretty picnic spot today.

Happily, the citizens soon rebuilt the cathedral which Montfort's troops had pillaged, producing a beautiful building which they continued to enrich till the seventeenth century. Pope John XXII made Lavaur a bishopric in 1317. A clock placed on the town's fifteenth-century tower in 1523 was enlivened in 1604 by the addition of a jolly peasant, who still strikes every half hour. The bishopric disappeared at the Revolution, and the episcopal palace was torn down. In the nineteenth century the bishop's garden was transformed in the 'English' style, and nothing today is more pleasant than walking in it, looking out over the River Agout. From here you can admire the brilliant architecture of A. de Cransac, who designed the bridge of Saint-Roch in 1786, said to have the largest arch of its kind in the world (48.75 metres long).

Just beyond Saint-Sulpice the D630 northwest from Lavaur meets the N88, which runs for 29 kilometres southwest back to Toulouse. But the beauties of this region of the Languedoc are by no means exhausted. Haute-Garonne is not the largest *département* of France, but it is large enough, and a tongue licks its way for many kilometres southwest as far as the Haute-Pyrénées and Spain. *En route* are two outstanding sights that are well worth the longish trip, especially for those who relish the finest monastic architecture. The first is Saint-Gaudens, reached by way of a

The solitude of the hills around Lacaune, near Brassac.

This peaceful square at Lavaur belies its savage history, for the town was a stronghold of medieval heretics who were mercilessly slaughtered by the orthodox in 1211.

hundred or so kilometres of excellent road (the N117).

On the way, if you have time, pause at the ancient town of Muret, with its medieval and renaissance half-timbered houses and its superb church of Saint-Jacques. Just north of here, on the road to Seysses, Simon de Montfort defeated the Cathar Count Raymond VI of Toulouse in 1213 and his ally King Pedro II of Aragon, who fell in the battle. Further south is Martres-Tolosane, whose name derives from the many Christians martyred here by the Saracens. Over their cemetery was built a church, Sancta-Maria-de-Martyribus. Its successor, built in 1309, with a bell-tower modelled on that of Saint-Sernin, Toulouse, is dedicated to the leading martyr, St Vidian, who is honoured every Trinity Sunday by a mock battle between Christians and Saracens.

Left This monument at Muret, birthplace of Clément Ader, the 'father of aviation', illustrates the French gift for overstatement.

Right A shuttered château, tucked away in the countryside just outside Lavaur.

Left At Rieux, on a bend in the River Arize, an ancient house peeps shyly through the trees.

Above A superb site for the finest of the fortified churches of the Pyrenees, the former cathedral of Saint-Bertrand-de-Comminges.

Ten kilometres southwest you pass through Saint-Martory, with an eighteenth-century bridge crossing the River Garonne and boasting two gateways, as well as the remains of the Cistercian abbey of Bonnefont. The road turns due west to Saint-Gaudens, its aspect marred by the extraction of natural gas in the neighbourhood, but its romanesque church still preserving magical capitals, Aubusson tapestries and a notable organ, rebuilt by Cavaillé-Coll in 1828.

Nobody quite knows when St Gaudens himself was martyred, or who did it: the Visigoths, the Saracens or the Vandals. But in 1309 Pope Clement VI, who had been Bishop of Comminges, pronounced that anyone visiting St Gauden's shrine on his annual feast day would receive seven years and seven months' remission of purgatory, and those visiting the shrine at other times during the eight-day annual festival, one year and a hundred days, which helped the collegiate church to flourish and kept the saint's name alive.

Saint-Gaudens is, however, merely a prelude to the greatest of the Pyrenees churches, the cathedral of Saint-Bertrand-de-Comminges. You reach it by driving 14 kilometres west to Montréjeau – with its arcaded square and fountain and its panoramic view of the Pyrenees – and then 10 kilometres south.

The site of Saint-Bertrand-de-Comminges was once an important Roman centre; the provincial governor Herod and his wife Herodias were exiled to this remote spot by the Emperor Caligula, and Roman baths, a temple, a forum and a theatre have been excavated here. The fortified medieval village is lovely; the twelfth-century church of Saint-Just-Saint-Pastor in the lower town is remarkable (its builders cannibalized columns from old Roman buildings); but the cathedral of Saint-Bertrand is magnificent. Its site dominates the valley of the Garonne. Its romanesque west end and narthex date from 1140; the great gothic nave was built in the first half of the fourteenth century. Those who

A fifteenth-century half-timbered house at Saint-Bertrand-de-Comminges.

added to its furnishings were clearly inspired by this superb house of God, for the early sixteenth century choir stalls are unsurpassed elsewhere in France. The stained glass is renaissance, the tapestries Aubusson. St Bertrand himself lies in a huge fifteenth-century shrine behind the high altar.

A very enjoyable round trip back to Toulouse takes in part of the *département* of Ariège, reached by retracing your steps through Montréjeau and Saint-Gaudens to Saint-Martory. Just south of Saint-Martory at Salies-du-Salat the Romans developed thermal baths, a fact rendered more piquant by the knowledge that the modern thermal establishment, built in 1923, was given neo-Egyptian frescoes for a film in the early part of this century. Those who walk inside hoping to cure rheumatism or stunted growth meet Cleopatra.

From here the route runs southeast past Saint-Lizier, the brick belfry of its romanesque cathedral a reminder that this region is still under the powerful architectural influence of Toulouse. Saint-Lizier is just north of Saint-Girons. Fifteen kilometres northeast of Saint-Girons is one of the most remarkable prehistoric caves in the whole of the Languedoc, the Mas-d'Azil, which can be visited. A vast underground tunnel, often 80 metres high, follows the course of the subterranean River Arize for 420 metres. Prehistoric man painted prehistoric animals and designs on its walls. The town hall museum in Le Mas d'Azil nearby displays the skulls and bones of bears and mammoths who took refuge in the cavern. Christians also sheltered here in the third century and their primitive chapel was used again by persecuted Cathars in the thirteenth century and by Protestants in the eighteenth.

Drive 20 or so kilometres southeast to reach Foix. The Ariège meets the Arget here and almost inevitably in this part of France this strategic site was occupied early, by a tenth-century abbey and then by a château. The latter still dominates the town, with its round battlemented keep and two square towers (one of them wearing a green, pointed hat), while the abbey church of Saint-Volusien has been much transformed since its first building.

From Foix back to Toulouse is a drive of 72

Left The view up the spectacular Garonne valley from Saint-Bertrand-de-Comminges.

Above **Autumn glory near Fronsac.**

49

Left The caves at Le Mas-d'Azil, which have provided shelter for prehistoric mammoths, persecuted early Christians, harried Cathars and hunted Protestants.

Above The cylindrical keep and the two square towers of the old château still dominate the sometime Cathar refuge of Foix.

kilometres northwest. The chief town *en route* is Pamiers, a centre for winter sports in the Pyrenees, and another city boasting a former cathedral massively influenced by the churches of Toulouse (though it did not in fact receive its final shape until the seventeenth century). Pamiers is a big city, bursting its seams for centuries (or so it appears from the houses set in its walls). But smaller places on the way are also well worth pausing for and you may be lucky enough to see a shepherd on a summer evening, carrying a crook, bringing home his sheep with the help of a couple of black sheepdogs.

Half-way between Pamiers and Toulouse is Auterive, with a massive brick church next to the market. Jeanne, Countess of Toulouse, sister-in-law of St Louis, built it in 1271, with a typically bizarre gothic gable. Inside on the left is a statue of the Trinity – a rare sight in Catholic churches, since the Council of Trent condemned them as likely to mislead the faithful about the true relationship between God the Father, God the Son and God the Holy Spirit. The name of the town, situated high on the bank of the Ariège, derives from the Latin *alta ripa* (high bank). This was modified into Haulterive and then Aulterive, reaching its present form only in the nineteenth century.

As a final treat if you are nearing Toulouse before sunset, make a small detour left along the D24 to Plaisance-du-Touch. The abbot of Bonnefont founded this bastide in 1275, so as to have a country seat within easy distance of Toulouse. The thirteenth-century church of Saint-Barthélemy is still here.

But the special treat is a 5-hectare park where over 250 animals roam in freedom. You can hug monkeys, stare at elephants, talk to parakeets, startle zebras and warily watch tigers. In this reconstructed garden of Eden you can picnic safely inside the perimeter fence. Or if it is growing late, you can drive the 10 kilometres back to Toulouse for a *cassoulet landais* made from the heart, neck, shoulder and liver of a duck, all delicately flavoured with sorrel.

The high Pyrenees.

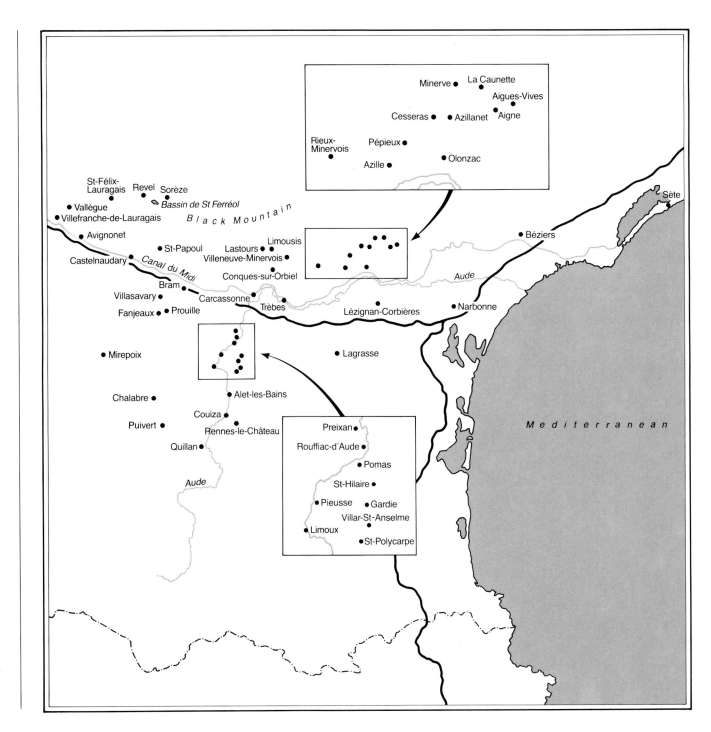

Minerve • La Caunette

Aigues-Vives

Cesseras • Azillanet • Aigne

Rieux-Minervois

Pépieux •

Azille • Olonzac

St-Félix-Lauragais

Revel Sorèze

• Vallègue *Bassin de St Ferréol*

• Villefranche-de-Lauragais *Black Mountain*

• Avignonet

• St-Papoul Limousis

Lastours

Villeneuve-Minervois

Béziers

Castelnaudary *Canal du Midi*

Conques-sur-Orbiel

Aude

Bram •

Villasavary • Carcassonne

Fanjeaux • Prouille Trèbes Lézignan-Corbières • Narbonne

Sète

• Mirepoix • Lagrasse

Mediterranean

Chalabre • Alet-les-Bains

Couiza Preixan

Puivert • Rouffiac-d'Aude •

Rennes-le-Château • Pomas

Quillan • St-Hilaire •

Aude • Pieusse • Gardie

Villar-St-Anselme

• Limoux

• St-Polycarpe

54

2
Dream Cities of the Midi

Carcassonne – Limoux – Fanjeaux – Prouille –
Mirepoix – Rennes-le-Château – Castelnaudary –
Lastours – Minerve

Everyone has a dream of the perfect medieval city: walled, with towers; a moat; knights jousting; an exquisite church, glittering stained glass in its gothic windows; bastions from which brave men poured lead on besiegers in times of assault. Such places do not exist outside Hollywood – save at Carcassonne.

The spectacular medieval city of Carcassonne, the largest fortified citadel in Europe, stands high on a hill 150 metres above the River Aude. It is almost certain that this place was called 'Carcaso' by a Celtic tribe two centuries before Christ, so the name is very ancient. The Romans built a hillfort here which stood on the wine road that joined Narbonne and Toulouse. The fort was still standing when Alaric the Goth sacked Rome in the fifth century AD, and when the Visigoths hid booty from Rome here after their conquest of Languedoc.

In 725 the growing town was taken by the Saracens and renamed Karkashuna. Even the Emperor Charlemagne failed to retake it for the French. Legend has it that he was tricked into calling off his siege when the Muslim princess Carcas stuffed the inhabitants' dwindling store of maize into their last surviving pig and flung it over the wall. Concluding that Carcassonne must be extraordinarily well-supplied with provisions, Charlemagne and his troops departed. But as the emperor rode away, the Muslim trumpets began to sound. Hearing 'Carcas sound' (Carcassonne), Charlemagne turned back and concluded a peace treaty with the beleaguered princess. Carcassonne became a bastion of Christianity against the Muslims.

History becomes clearly separable from legend again in the twelfth century when the Viscounts Trencavel of Béziers proclaimed themselves Viscounts of Carcassonne as well. They ruled the city for a century, also dominating Albi, Béziers, Nîmes and the surrounding countryside. The first viscount, Bernard Aton, fought the Muslims in Spain and in the Holy Land. His successors continued to build and enrich the city and to patronize the musicians and artists, in particular the troubadours. Princess Adelaide of Burlats, for instance, for whom Arnaud de Mareuil was supposedly dying of love (though he also sang of his courtly love for the ladies of Montpellier) was married to a Viscount of Carcassonne.

In the mid twelfth century the citizens of Carcassonne accepted a Cathar named Guiraud Mercier as their bishop. Catharism soon had a powerful grip on the city, sheltered by Adelaide's husband, Roger II Trencavel, who for a time was excommunicated by the pope. In 1204 the King of Aragon even presided here at an amicable debate between the Catholics and the Cathars.

Such mutual tolerance did not last. After the defeat

55

of the Cathars of Béziers in 1209, the Catholic crusaders reached Carcassonne on 1 August. In spite of the desperate bravery of the heretics, the Catholics managed to breach the great walls. The Viscount of Carcassonne, aged only twenty-four, surrendered himself on condition his people were spared. Burying their treasure inside the city (some of it has been found in this century), the rest of the inhabitants fled carrying only the clothes they stood up in, 'shirts and trousers' as the chronicle has it. The viscount was incarcerated in one of the towers of his own city and died miserably on 10 November, his young son safe under the protection of the Count of Foix. Simon de Montfort became Lord of Carcassonne.

After de Montfort's death, Count Raymond VII of Toulouse and the Count of Foix drove out his son and made the seventeen-year-old Raymond Trencavel Viscount of Carcassonne. Soon both he and Raymond of Toulouse were excommunicated. King Louis VII of France marched south in support of the Montforts, and long before he reached Carcassonne its citizens sent delegates offering him the city.

Trencavel fled to Aragon. The Montforts took over the city again; the dubiously orthodox bishop was replaced; and the people began to repair the defences. This time they built a double defensive ring of walls and turrets. When Raymond Trencavel returned in force in 1240, his attack was a complete failure.

Finally, in the 1270s and 1280s Kings Philippe II the Bold and Philippe IV the Fair massively strengthened the already powerful defences of their city, now a major bulwark of their kingdom against Spain. So inviolable did Carcassonne seem at this time that it came to be called 'the maid of the Languedoc'. Even the Black Prince, who set fire to the *ville basse* or lower town in 1355, wisely declined to attack the old *cité*.

Small wonder then that visitors have marvelled at the old city of Carcassonne. Only Paris itself and Mont-Saint-Michel attract more visitors every year. 'No other town can present so vivid and clean-cut a fossil of the seven hundred years into which poured and melted all the dissolution of antiquity, and out of which was formed and crystallized the highly specialized diversity of our modern Europe,' judged Hilaire Belloc in 1906. Carcassonne, he wrote, differs from other monumental towns in that it 'preserves exactly the aspect of many centuries up to a certain moment, and from that moment has "set", and has suffered no further change.'

That acute and extremely intelligent traveller was for once completely wrong. Far from being 'set' in the Middle Ages, the old city of Carcassonne gradually went into decline in the seventeenth century. The Peace of the Pyrenees in 1659 annexed Roussillon to France and as a result the Spanish border was now much further south. A powerful defensive citadel was no longer needed here and the growing prosperity of the region enriched not the old city but the suburb which had developed from the thirteenth century as the *ville basse*. Its cathedral was even more important than the beautiful gothic cathedral of Saint-Nazaire inside the citadel walls. Parts of the old city slowly became derelict. In 1850 it was decided to demolish all that remained of the redundant fortifications.

Fortunately the supreme gothic architect of nineteenth-century France had begun work restoring the basilica of Saint-Nazaire in 1844, which had been used to store fodder during the Revolution. He joined forces with a local archaeologist, Jean-Pierre Cros-Mayrevielle, to save old Carcassonne and they enlisted the help of the distinguished man of letters, Prosper Mérimée, who was also inspector of historic monuments. In 1855 Viollet-le-Duc began work on the restoration of the medieval fortifications, work that was to be triumphantly brought to a conclusion by his pupil Boeswillwald and his admirer Nodet.

The authenticity of the work has been much disputed. Viollet-le-Duc was a northern architect who, it is said, failed to grasp the essence of medieval Languedoc. One recent French guide-book describes modern Carcassonne as 'a Romano-Visigothic-feudal coproduction, presented by Viollet-le-Duc'. Henry James judged better. On the vexed question of

The dream city of Carcassonne.

restoration in general he declared himself as one who invariably preferred the ruined, however ruined, to the reconstructed, however splendid. The one, he wrote, is history; the other fiction. And this great novelist found history far more romantic than fiction. Then he added: 'After that I am free to say that the restoration of Carcassonne is a splendid achievement.'

For my part, I agree with Henry James's assessment of Viollet-le-Duc's work, but I disagree with his view on the relative merits of the tumbledown and the restored. Throughout history ancient buildings have been lovingly restored, so long as people did love them. Unloved Carcassonne desperately needed loving restoration, and Viollet-le-Duc gave it just that. As for his supposed lack of feel for the architecture of southern France, the truth is that he was wise enough to gather together a group of local workmen: masons, stone-cutters, blacksmiths, carpenters and sculptors. These were 'men all used to difficult jobs', as he put it, 'and all working on the site under my direction'.

Today architects have replaced some of his roofing slates with the flat tiles that scholars tell us were used for thirteenth-century royal buildings here; but as more objective eyes explore the work of the great nineteenth-century gothicist, scholars are also realizing how well Viollet-le-Duc utilized what he could of the old work, his principal aim (apart from restoration) being to stop everything falling into ruins.

The drive to the walled city from the *ville basse* is a breathtakingly romantic experience. From the gate near the cathedral of the *ville basse* drive left and then sharp right, looking out for signposts marked *cité*. As you cross the River Aude over the old bridge, the massive walls rise ahead. Not even the overpriced cafés and restaurants, the artists' studios and the bric-à-brac of tourism can spoil its charm. With some imagination the youth hostel might almost be said to represent the old welcome given to pilgrims, and the mummers and street musicians the tradition of the troubadours.

Carcassonne boasts 3 kilometres of ramparts, bristling with thirty-five defensive towers. Nineteen of the towers protect the outer ramparts, which are built down the hill from the inner ones, allowing

The porte Narbonnaise with its fronting moat, vital protection on this side of Carcassonne.

attackers to be repulsed from two levels at once. In between them are the *lices* (used as tiltyards in peace time – *lices* has given us the English word lists), which offered deadly open spaces to an enemy who scaled or penetrated the outer ramparts. 'Nowhere else in Europe does there exist such a complete and formidable array of defence work,' wrote Viollet-le-Duc.

You park outside the fortress-like porte Narbonnaise, built on the orders of Philippe the Bold to defend the eastern entrance to the *cité*, its bossed stones designed to ricochet arrows back on the enemy. By far the most powerful of the city gates, the porte Narbonnaise was vital protection for the least defensible slope of the site of Carcassonne. (Compare the lie of the land here, for example, with that outside the porte d'Aude to the west of the *cité*, where defence was much easier.) On the right of the porte

Narbonnaise rises the blue-tiled treasury tower, also built by Philippe the Bold.

Only when you walk up to the viscounts' castle (the Château Comtal) do you realize that you are in fact inside a real city, with small houses and narrow streets, as well as inside a mighty fortification. The castle itself is a fortress within a fortress – defended by its moat and gates from any enemy who might have taken the rest of the *cité*. Viollet-le-Duc reconstructed the medieval wooden 'hoardings', with their trapdoors for dropping missiles on attackers. A guided tour of the castle reveals yet more fortifications, including those of the Visigoths, whose towers are decorated with fine bands of thin red brick. In the round chamber is a fresco representing a battle between the Franks and the Saracens.

From the château wander through the *cité* to its greatest architectural treasure (but one which closes midday for the traditional two-hour lunch): the glorious basilica of Saint-Nazaire. Part romanesque with a thirteenth-century gothic transept and apse, its first stones were blessed by Pope Urban II in 1096. Viollet-le-Duc's masterly restoration was completed in 1898.

The central window of the apse is filled with fourteenth-century stained glass, flanked by two sixteenth-century windows. Adjoining them on either side of the apse are two windows with more early fourteenth-century glass containing scenes from the lives of St Peter and St Paul and from the lives of St Nazaire and his mother St Celse. The superb glass in the south rose window, depicting Christ in majesty, can be precisely dated from the coat of arms of Bishop Pierre de Rochefort, who was Bishop of Carcassonne from 1300 to 1321.

Simon de Montfort's tomb, representing the knight and the lion of Montfort, is in the south transept, though his body is not, having been removed to Montfort l'Amaury just west of Paris. And in the chapel of the Sacred Heart is a remarkable crudely carved 'siege-stone' dating from the early thirteenth century. In the top right-hand corner an angel carries the soul of a soldier killed in the siege to heaven. Could

the 'siege-stone' of Carcassonne depict the death of Simon de Montfort outside the walls of Toulouse in 1218?

Finally walk south of the church to the tower of Saint-Nazaire. Here I have often brooded on the mighty bulwarks of the impregnable 'maid of the Languedoc'. The views are stupendous and an orientation table sets out what can be seen in the remarkable panorama stretching before you.

After exploring such a superb city, the prospect of the *ville basse* of Carcassonne might not seem so enticing. But it is in fact equally rewarding. St Louis of France (Louis IX) built the lower city in 1260 as a walled bastide, with a checkerboard pattern of streets. The inhabitants of the suburbs of Saint-Michel and Saint-Vincent, which had grown up outside the walls of the *cité*, flocked into the *ville basse*. Although the Black Prince razed it in 1355, the *ville basse* was immediately rebuilt on a scarcely reduced scale. Modern boutiques, restaurants and hotels have in no way diminished its charm.

If you arrive at the station (or stay as I have done at the hotel opposite), explore the lower city by walking from the station along the shady pedestrianized rue George-Clemenceau, with its shops and supermarket. On the left you pass the thirteenth-century Carmelite church, which boasts modern stained glass representing Elijah rising to heaven from Mount Carmel in a flaming chariot.

Just beyond is place Carnot, a tree-lined market square sporting a splendid Neptune fountain put here in 1770. Going south from here, rue Court-Jarre takes you past the excellent modern municipal theatre as far as the mighty walls of the lower city.

Just inside the city walls, rue Voltaire leads west to the medieval cathedral of Saint-Michel. Since the old suburbs of the *cité* had been dedicated to Saint-Michel and Saint-Vincent, the pious King Louis charged his subjects to build two churches dedicated to these saints in his new bastide. This is one of them. In superb condition (partly owing to Viollet-le-Duc's work in 1849, partly owing to enlightened patrons of the twentieth century), Saint-Michel is a beautiful

example of languedocien gothic church architecture, i.e. a single nave with a series of vaulted chapels on either side. After the Black Prince's depredations the church became part of the city ramparts, so that the outside looks more like a fortress than a house of God.

If you explore the outside you can in fact trace where old entrances have been blocked up. The main doorway was once in the rue Voltaire on the north side of the church – an unusual position, but designed to keep out the southeasterly rains blowing in from the sea and the cold northwesterly winds. In 1950, when the present west doorway was pierced, the cathedral authorities decided worshippers should put up with the winds to give access to a fine garden.

Saint-Michel became a cathedral only in 1803. Then a fire of 1849 gave the ubiquitous Viollet-le-Duc the chance to make the interior worthy of its newly exalted status. He left the high altar of 1740, but the choir stalls are his and he decided that the organ which the Parisian Jean de Joyeuse had built in 1684 caused 'more scandal than edification'. The brilliant organ builder Aristide Cavaillé-Coll was called on to design a magnificent three-manual instrument of 208 stops and 3360 pipes. As a result, Sunday worship at Saint-Michel is a thrilling experience, even for unbelievers.

Unfortunately Cavaillé-Coll's organ is so massive that it almost totally conceals the splendid rose window in the west wall. If you can, look at the window from the garden after dark, when the stained glass is subtly lit from the inside. The central window of the choir, consisting of fourteenth-century fragments pieced together, is also best seen in this way.

The *ville basse* of Carcassonne is a city to saunter in. From the cathedral stroll back towards the railway station along rue Docteur Albert-Tomey, with its dress-shops, bakers and a pâtisserie. You pass a classical market hall where a colourful market operates on Saturdays and then the high bell-tower of the church of Saint-Vincent comes into view – battle-

This carving in the rue Barbes in the lower city of Carcassonne pays tribute to the towers of the upper city.

mented, with gothic arches over a romanesque base.

Whereas the cathedral belfry makes do with 6 bells, Saint-Vincent boasts a carillon of no fewer than 47. This lovely languedocien gothic church is the second widest in France (after Mirepoix) and its dimensions are what make it a masterpiece.

Incredibly, it survived transformation into a foundry at the time of the Revolution, housing several forges and piles of coke. (The outrage involved makes one quite glad that the poet and Revolutionary Fabre d'Eglantine, who was born at Carcassonne in 1750, was guillotined as a Dantonist in 1794). The stained glass did not survive the transformation, but in my view the choir windows, dating from 1883, are an excellent attempt at copying fifteenth-century glass. The pulpit and the paintings date from the eighteenth century (my favourite, in the chapel of Saint-Joan-of-Arc, is a

The magnificent Neptune fountain in place Carnot, one of the attractions of the *ville basse*, Carcassonne.

61

LANGUEDOC

painting by Pierre Subleyras of St Jerome receiving communion); and underneath the organ are four fourteenth-century statues (in fairly miserable condition), one of which is the sole authentic portrait of St Louis, founder of the *ville basse*.

When the church reverted to its proper use, one grisly touch added a new element of sanctity. St Hemenès, an athlete who had turned Christian, had lain in the cemetery of Saint Callistus, Rome, since his martyrdom in the third century. In 1877 he was dug up and brought here. His wax-covered, dressed-up corpse now lies in the chapel of Saint-Roch, half-way up the church. (The church also possesses what is claimed to be a hand of St Anne, Jesus's grandmother.)

There are other lovely churches in the *ville basse*, particularly the flamboyant gothic Notre-Dame-de-la-Sainté. If you continue along rue Docteur Albert-Tomey you reach a grim city bastion (these days giving protection to a children's playground) and turn right to reach the railway station again.

The hotel I stayed in when I last visited Carcassonne overlooked some locks on the Canal du Midi, and I would sit on my balcony as the evening sun finally set, watching five or so boats tying up and a couple of hitch-hiking students wrapping themselves in sleeping-bags to bed down on the grassy canal bank.

The Canal du Midi is the brilliant realization of a centuries-old dream by one man, Pierre-Paul Riquet, Baron of Bonrepos. According to Tacitus, Augustus Caesar wanted to construct a canal through the isthmus of Gaul. So did Charlemagne. Neither accomplished it. In 1539 François I conceived the notion of a canal to join the rivers Aude and Garonne and Henri IV subsequently discussed the idea in 1598; but nothing was achieved. And a plan by an engineer called Bernard Arribat to construct a waterway between Toulouse and Narbonne in the reign of Louis XIII was universally opposed in the region, simply because no-one believed that such a canal could be properly supplied with water all the year round. The financial implications of such a huge project were also impossibly daunting.

By 1660 Pierre-Paul Riquet was farmer-general of salt-taxes throughout Languedoc-Roussillon. He was also contractor for the royal army, continually engaged in conflict with Spain. As a result of his own difficulties in travelling the vast region, he became interested in the notion of a canal, even though his father, a Béziers lawyer, had been one of those responsible for turning down the plans of Bernard Arribat.

Riquet's château at Bonrepos was not far from the Black Mountain, with its abundant springs. He discussed his plans with Pierre Campas, the fountain-maker of Revel, who taught him the 'lore of springs'. He also sought the advice of a mathematician named Pierre Petit on the problems of supplying enough water for a canal 16 metres wide and 2 metres deep between Carcassonne and Toulouse. The plan he came up with was to divert streams from the Black Mountain to the north to the pass of Naurouze – at 189 metres above sea-level this was higher than any point that would be reached by the proposed canal and thus water could be channelled from here towards either the Aude or the Garonne.

Riquet enlisted the support of the Archbishop of Toulouse, who in turn put the plans to Louis XIV's powerful minister Colbert, just when Colbert himself was attempting a massive expansion of French trade. Colbert called Riquet to Paris to discuss the idea of bringing a canal from the port of Sète as far as Beaucaire. Riquet visited the Briare natural park in the Loire to study the scheme of locks on its many waterways and then returned to the Languedoc to dig a trial canal from Revel to Naurouze at his own expense. In October 1666 Louis XIV signed an edict commanding 'the building of a navigable canal between the Mediterranean sea and the Ocean' without delay.

Riquet set in motion an enterprise that involved '12,000 heads' (with a man reckoned as one head and three women as two!), using picks and spades. Work

The Canal du Midi near Carcassonne, once crowded with barges carrying grain, now a paradise for canal-cruisers.

62

began in 1667 and ended only fourteen years later. The whole undertaking cost 17,161,028 livres. A reservoir was constructed at Saint-Ferréol containing seven million cubic metres of water. From Sète to Toulouse the canal rises 56 metres through 64 locks, some of them with 8 sets of gates, most of them 30 metres long (though a good number have been enlarged since Riquet's time). At Malpas the canal was obliged to pass underground through a tunnel 165 metres long.

Riquet was sixty when the work began, and he wore out himself and his fortune in seeing it through. Exhausted and utterly impoverished, he died at Toulouse on 1 October 1680 when the canal needed only about 5 kilometres to reach the sea. Another engineer, Paul Mathias, had to connect Riquet's canal to Beaucaire, by means of the Canal du Rhône. On May 15 the following year the first twenty-three barges left the Garonne, loaded with goods for the fair at Beaucaire.

In 1684 barges were charged sixty sous a day for the eight days sailing between Agde and Toulouse. Grain was the principal cargo, carried south from Toulouse to the Mediterranean. In July the fair at Beaucaire crammed the locks with barges. And today tourism means that the waterway remains a major asset to the Languedoc.

Others besides Mathias (including Louis XIV's great military architect Vauban) added to and extended Riquet's work. Toulouse was connected to Bordeaux by a canal in 1856. The splendid aqueduct over the River Orb at Béziers dates from 1857. A new dam built in the Black Mountain in 1948 reserved a further four million cubic metres of water for the canal.

But essentially the achievement was Riquet's. Ironically, when Arthur Young saw the canal in the late eighteenth century, though ecstatic, he gave the credit to Riquet's royal master.

'Leave the road,' he urged his readers, 'and crossing the canal, follow it to Béziers; nine sluice gates let the water down the hill to join the river at the town. A noble work! The port is broad enough for four large vessels to lie abreast; the greatest of them carries from 90 to 100 tons. Many of them were at the quay, some in motion, and every sign of an animated business. This is the best sight I have seen in France. Here Louis XIV thou art truly great!'

Quite apart from the engineering achievement involved and its economic importance to the Languedoc, the Canal du Midi is beautiful, with its gracefully elliptical locks, its elegant late seventeenth-century bridges, and the 45,000 oaks, plane trees, cypresses, pines and poplars that line its banks. (Riquet also planted olive trees and mulberry bushes, but these have all gone.) Today it is used chiefly by holidaymakers who rent canal-cruisers and cover, say, 130 of its 240 kilometres in a week. I think the finest part for this leisurely life stretches 100 kilometres or so from Carcassonne to the seventeenth-century staircase locks that Young so admired at Béziers.

If you are still travelling by road, leave Carcassonne south by the D118 for Limoux, driving alongside the River Aude through 24 kilometres of enchanting countryside. On the right the red tiles of the village of Preixan climb up to its church.

You drive through Rouffiac-d'Aude, which takes its name from Ruffiacus, the Roman centurion who founded it in the third century AD. Across the river appears the charming village of Pomas, with its thirteenth-century château (with fifteenth-century mullions) and a gothic church which boasts seventeenth-century painted and gilded statues of the Virgin Mary and St Roch. The sunlight flickers through arcades of plane trees, from which you emerge to drive through hectares of vineyards. Nearly all the grapes here are destined for that excellent sparkling pale yellow wine known as *Blanquette de Limoux*, created out of a judicious mixture of Mauzac, Chardonnay and Chenin grapes.

A huge and entertaining ceramic depicting the citizens of Limoux welcomes you as you reach the town, but before exploring further, make a detour left, where the sign points to Saint-Hilaire. Cross the River

Crumbling plaster and fading shutters in the lazy town of Arques, southeast of Limoux.

Aude and continue following the signs – quite suddenly, at a bend in the road, you will see the fourteenth-century basilica of Notre-Dame-de-Marceille. There is a shady picnic spot to park in at the far side of the church. Over the doorway is a gorgeous coloured fifteenth-century Madonna, blessed by two angels bearing censers; the door itself has a stupendous multiple lock; and the church is packed with treasures, not least a romanesque 'Black Virgin', a fourteenth-century pulpit, and the fifteenth-century Madonna and Child which made this spot a place of pilgrimage for centuries.

This is a good spot to have a picnic lunch before driving on through Pieusse and along a road that winds through gentle rolling hillside, vines and broom, trees and shrub, with the occasional house dotted here and there till you reach the little village of Saint-Hilaire. Saint-Hilaire grew around a Benedictine abbey founded in 550 by St Hilaire himself, the first Bishop of Carcassonne. The village, peaceful today, is still fortified, and rue du Pont-Levis (the street of the drawbridge) leads round the back of the church to the gentle abbey cloisters, with a well and slender double pillars.

The monks of Saint-Hilaire were the first to make *Blanquette de Limoux*. Much meditation must have gone into perfecting the technique, for the process is complex enough. The grapes are first pressed to produce a strictly regulated maximum of 100 litres of must from each 150 kilograms of grapes. The must is then left in vats for twelve hours, before being drawn off into new vats in order to ferment at a temperature of 20°C for up to three weeks. The wine is racked to produce a perfectly clear liquid, and then kept over winter. Blending takes place the following spring, the cuvée is bottled, and a second fermentation takes place over nine months in cellars where the temperature is kept between 9° and 13°C. Next the bottles are laid on shaking tables (called 'riddlers'), and are turned daily by hand so that the deposit sets itself against the cork.

The thirteenth-century keep of the partly-ruined château still broods outside Arques.

When this process is complete the cork is abruptly removed and the deposit comes out with it. Finally a little wine is drawn out of each bottle. It is replaced with wine from the same cuvée mixed with a few carefully-measured centilitres of sugar-cane to produce Brut, Demi-Sec, or Demi-Doux. Not surprisingly after all this care, the vintners tell you you must only drink *Blanquette de Limoux* at a temperature of 6° to 8°C. If you climb the steps at the corner of the cloister in Saint-Hilaire to the former gaol-house, you can taste and buy the wine, as well as the spirited Corbières honey made in the village.

The present abbey church, which dates from the twelfth century, has a contemporary marble sarcophagus of the founder. This is not decorated with scenes from his life but depicts St Saturninus, dragged by the bull, his soul being received into heaven (see Chapter 1).

The church at Saint-Hilaire is well cared for, and in summer always filled with arrangements of sunflowers. In the roof vaults the hand of God blesses us, Jesus is represented as the Lamb of God and there is a blank for the Holy Spirit. One charming feature is that St James the Great, dressed as always for his perpetual pilgrimage to Compostela, has a dog to keep him company.

Returning towards Limoux, you take the first turning on the left to follow the D151 as far as Gardie, where the clock on the gothic church belfry passes the time of day and the war memorial tells you that eight sons of this remote village died in World War I, three of them called Lacube and two of them called Deloupy. Continue as far as the D51 and turn right to drive 5 kilometres to Saint-Polycarpe by way of the hilltop village of Villar-Saint-Anselme. Around the corner the massive, blind, fortified church of Notre-Dame suddenly appears. Standing here since the eleventh century, it was once the abbey church of a Benedictine monastery founded two centuries earlier.

Ahead are wooded mountains, sheltering the town of Alet-les-Bains at a height of 650 metres. If the legend is to be believed, this protection proved vital in the Middle Ages. The story is that an ill-tempered giant

named Marre who lived at Saint-Polycarpe threw a huge boulder at Alet-les-Bains, which fortunately buried itself in the mountainside.

Under the high altar in the church are a couple of lovely fourteenth-century silver-gilt reliquaries, one bearing pieces of the body of St Polycarp (who was burnt at the stake at Smyrna in 156) and the other of St Benedict (who died at Monte Cassino in 550). It would be churlish to doubt the relics' authenticity. On either side are two ninth-century Carolingian altars, with subtly interlaced carvings – on one a Greek cross displays the letters alpha and omega.

Take the D129 and drive 6 kilometres east to Limoux. The old bridge at Limoux was built in the sixteenth century, but is known as the *pont neuf* (since there is another one a century older). Crossing the Aude by this bridge will bring you directly to the splendid ensemble created by the gothic church and slender stone spire of the cathedral of Saint-Martin. Indeed, the whole city is delightful, with picturesque streets and half-timbered houses. The place de la République, arcaded on three sides, is an old covered market square with a sweetly decadent, topless lady and two cherubs decorating its fountain. (Four other cherubs blow horns that spurt out water.)

Gastronomically Limoux is remarkable. Pepper cakes (*gâteau au poivre* – in *langue d'oc, fogassets al pebre*) are made here, which help to stimulate a thirst for more *Blanquette de Limoux*. Another remarkable mixture, known as *la fricassée de Limoux*, is served in two dishes. One holds white beans with their skins; the other a fricassée made from diced pork with bits of ham, liver, kidneys, heart, sweetbread, spleen and knucklebone, all cooked in a rich sauce. Mix them together on your plate and wash them down with a ripe red wine.

I have grown to like this mixture, provided that the accompanying wine is strong enough to match it. But if it is too rough for your taste, try the superb snail stew they serve in this region (*civet d'escargots de Limoux*). This includes onions, garlic and mushrooms (either the ones called *lactaires* or *champignons de Paris*) and is cooked with red wine. If you stay for a second meal, try the local duck (*canard à la limouxine*), flavoured with saffron and whole grains of garlic.

The Roman spa of Alet-les-Bains lies 9 kilometres further south and is the most important thermal resort in these parts. Local historians claim that Charlemagne himself cured his indigestion by taking the waters here. Turn left along its medieval walls (dilapidated but still standing) and drive along narrow streets with overhanging half-timbered houses to the arcaded place de la République. In 1573 the Huguenots ruined the town's old twelfth-century cathedral, and it was never rebuilt. (A cemetery now occupies part of the ruins, and the former episcopal palace has become a hotel.)

Seven kilometres south of Alet-les-Bains, turn left at Couiza with its lovely renaissance château. The terrain becomes rockier, slightly ominous, matching the reputation of the village of Rennes-le-Château, where the legendary treasure of the Knights Templar is said to have been hidden.

In 1891 a parish priest named Bérengar Saunière is said to have found coded messages under the altar here, one of which read:

'TO DAGOBERT II, KING, AND TO SION, BELONGS THIS TREASURE, AND HE IS THERE DEAD'

Even more surprisingly, Saunière began to spend vast amounts of money in 1896, far more than his meagre salary would allow. The Bishop of Carcassonne demanded an explanation of his wealth; an explanation was refused; the bishop suspended the priest; Saunière appealed to the Vatican and was reinstated.

On 17 January 1919 he suffered a stroke. A fellow priest came to hear his last confession. He left the sick man's bedroom totally shaken. Saunière died five days later, unshriven. His will revealed that he was penniless. But before his death he had restored the church at Rennes-le-Château, erecting a statue of the devil Asmodeus inside the door and incising the

The *pont neuf* in Limoux, spanning the River Aude and leading towards the cathedral of Saint-Martin.

Above **A dog wonders whether to explore the church at Couiza.**

Right **Between Couiza and Quillan a graceful seventeenth-century bridge spans the river at Campagne-sur-Aude.**

Puffing and panting, medieval timbers support the arcades at Mirepoix.

legend TERRIBILIS EST LOCUS ISTE (this place is terrible) over the doorway.

Rennes-le-Château is only 4.5 kilometres from Couiza but the panorama *en route* is extraordinary: bleak, with scarcely a vine; red outcrops of rock, then white outcrops; distant blue mountains, nearer green ones; scarcely any human habitation, save remote châteaux, until you reach the village itself. Here, in Bérengar Saunière's garden, you can eat an ice-cream and enjoy a *frisson* of historical fantasy. And it is certainly startling when you enter the church to have holy water presented to you on the back of a leering hideous devil.

Return to Couiza and follow the D118 south to Quillan – though an industrial town, it is blessed with fine old houses on the banks of the Aude and a seventeenth-century bridge crossing it.

The route from here now runs northwest for 16 kilometres to Puivert, whose château appears ahead dominating the ridge. Though partly ruined, Puivert château still has its powerful keep (35 metres high) and some impressive walls, as well as a couple of fairly fearsome great halls. People swim in the lake at Puivert, though I have not.

Eight kilometres north the delightful village of Chalabre lies on the rivulet known as the Blau, over which hang pretty (if tumbledown) houses. Dominating the village is a château built in the fifteenth century and after, around a twelfth-century keep. The statue in the village is that of one of Simon de Montfort's allies, Thomas II de Bruyers. And on a promontory to the north is a fourteenth-century calvary chapel, with very fine views.

From Chalabre follow the D18/D28 west until it hits the D625 and turn right to reach Mirepoix. The medieval gateway and narrow streets with overhanging houses here leave you quite unprepared for the huge central square with its great wooden arcades, a magical survival from the Middle Ages. Everything here is irregular. On one side of the square stands the former cathedral (the largest in the Midi), with the arcades continuing round its choir and a separate bell-tower. The citizens sit nonchalantly under the hanging lamps of the arcades, seemingly oblivious to the carved medieval faces of kings, nuns and animals who watch them. Yet they retain a good number of their old festivals – in particular the annual August feast of the Brotherhood of the White Penitents, when a whole street is set out with tables for a communal meal, bunting flies, men sing, and then everyone dances.

Four kilometres east of Mirepoix turn left and drive 27 kilometres north to Castelnaudary. The papal legate whose murder began the Albigensian crusade was born here. In 1355 the Black Prince destroyed the château and most of the town. Between here and Fresquel near Bram is where the Duke of Montmorency, executed at Toulouse in 1632, lost his final battle. It lasted only thirty minutes, and a hundred men died. The duke himself, riding his Arab grey, was first wounded in the neck; his horse fell dying,

The River Aude flows through Quillan, at the heart of the Corbières wine country.

Left South of Quillan, beyond Belvianes-et-Cavirac, the River Aude slices its way through the cliffs in the gorge of Pierre-Lys.

Above During the siesta at Mirepoix the hairdresser snoozes behind closed shutters.

crushing its rider, now bleeding from seventeen wounds. Pulled from under the animal, Montmorency was carried to a hut and made what seemed to be his final confession. So long as it seemed he would die of his wounds, Cardinal Richelieu spoke hypocritically of pardoning him of treason and sentencing him only to life imprisonment. When Montmorency's constitution pulled him through, his fate was sealed. Richelieu counselled the king to have the rebel beheaded.

But Castelnaudary today is remembered not so much for these grisly episodes as for its proud boast to have invented *cassoulet*. Some claim it happened during one of the sieges of the Hundred Years War, when all that was left in the beleaguered town were *haricots verts*, salt and fresh pork, some sheep, geese and old sausages. Others place the origin of the dish even earlier, when Simon de Montfort besieged the town in 1211. Whatever the date, haricots cannot have been included in the earliest *cassoulets*, since they were introduced from the New World only after 1492. Whether there is any truth in all this or not, every year the 'noble company of tasters of the *cassoulet* of Castelnaudary' solemnly dons its robes (in red, ermine and yellow) to proclaim the glories of this dish, which today is found throughout Languedoc.

Highly developed taste buds can distinguish regional varieties of *cassoulet*. Toulouse chefs use less pork and more sausage, and at Carcassonne they add a shoulder of mutton (or a mutton chop) and partridge. But the dishes are recognizably cousins. Today's *cassoulet* at Castelnaudary is made by boiling beans (preferably the variety known as *lingots*) in an earthenware pot for five minutes, throwing the water away, covering the beans with lukewarm water, adding large pieces of bacon rind, chitterling sausages, minced bacon with garlic, and simmering for two hours. Meanwhile a haunch of pork is browned in the fat of Lauragais goose. Everything is finally put in layers in a casserole (starting and ending with beans) and cooked carefully in an oven for three or four hours. An even brown crust is formed over the surface (and sometimes knocked into the mixture, so that a second and a third crust can be formed). The delicacy is served piping hot in the same casserole.

After a dish of *cassoulet* the visitor may not feel equal to exploring Castelnaudary, which would be a pity. The old quarter of the town boasts lovely, renaissance houses and pretty balconies. The thirteenth-century collegiate church of Saint-Michel has a splendid tower 50 metres high (carrying a carillon). It is wide enough for the street to run through it. On a nearby hill the seventeenth-century windmill has been restored to working order. The Monday market is a treat.

Eight kilometres northeast of Castelnaudary, along the D103, is the gorgeous former cathedral of Saint-Papoul. It seems incredible that this little village of fewer than 600 souls could once have been the seat of a bishop, but so it was after 1317 by decree of Pope John XXII. Earlier the cathedral church belonged to a Benedictine abbey, founded at Saint-Papoul in the eighth century on the tomb of a martyr of the same name (one of the followers of St Saturninus of Toulouse) who had his hermitage here. A nineteenth-century chapel marks the spot where his hermitage is thought to have stood, for there the pagans caught and martyred him. Pilgrims still come to venerate his memory on the last Sunday in April.

The church is fascinating – half romanesque, half gothic, with a twelfth-century choir and a fourteenth-century nave. Walk round the outside of the apse to admire the richly carved romanesque capitals. Amongst many ornaments inside the church (a Pietà, choir stalls, statuesque tombs) is the mausoleum of a seventeenth-century prelate, François de Donadieu, with a proud marble statue.

Equally delightful are the former abbey cloisters. It is hard to date them exactly, but they were probably built in the fourteenth century. Each arcade is supported by rows of twin columns, decorated with capitals. But the south wing is an oddity, with lovely

The collegiate church of Saint-Michel rises above the narrow streets of Castelnaudary, seen across a great basin of the Canal du Midi.

pink bricks instead of stone used for the columns. Were they all once like this, until the abbot and monks decided that the humble local brick was not good enough for them and imported stone instead?

Certainly the bishops lived sumptuously. Their palace, now a private dwelling, still stands in the nearby park along with the remains of the old monastery buildings. And the cathedral itself prospered with royal patronage, one of its treasures being a cope given by Catherine de Médicis. She and Charles IX are known to have visited the Château de Ferrals nearby, which François de Rougier began building in 1567. Although the château is not now open to visitors, it is well worth pausing as you drive northwest along the D126 from Saint-Papoul just to see the outside. Partly hidden among the trees, Château de Ferrals has a lovely tawny-yellow façade, defended at each corner by massive towers, as well as by a moat crossed by a powerful stone bridge. This leads to what was once the drawbridge, its gate again defended by a couple of round towers. François, it seems, knew enough about human treachery to take suitable precautions.

Continue northwest for another 25 kilometres until the T-junction with the D622, where you turn right for Revel, a bastide founded in 1342 by Philippe VI de Valois. The place Philippe-VI houses an entrancing covered market (with the tourist office in the hall in the middle). Strong thick wooden columns hold up the roof, the whole construction very low like a great canopy. The square is surrounded by shady arcading, the arches chiefly of stone, with beams here and there supporting a mixture of thin bricks and stone.

One Monday, after a sip of *liqueur de menthe* for which Revel is famous, I stood frustrated near the café outside a bookshop that was closed. I must have told my companion that I had been hoping to buy a recent history of the French Resistance in Haute-Garonne, which was on display in the window, for a chubby

The reservoir of Saint-Ferréol near Revel, a brilliant eighteenth-century engineering feat, created to feed the Canal du Midi.

man in his sixties with white stubble on his chin and a moistened eye began to tell me a tale. He must have been about sixty-five, for he said he was twenty-two when France capitulated. He and his eighteen-year-old brother had both joined the Resistance. One night, he recounted with graphic detail, he was in the forest with his rifle seeking Nazis when suddenly bullets began whistling by. 'Bim-boum', he cried, imitating their sound and indicating with his podgy old hands their trajectory on either side of his head. 'I decided to give in,' he recalled, 'even though it meant curtains for me.' He ostentatiously dropped his rifle and slowly turned round, his hands in the air – only to find that he was being mistakenly arrested by his own younger brother, also on the look-out for Nazis.

It is worth turning southeast again here for a couple of kilometres in order to drive around the north side of the Bassin de Saint-Ferréol, one of the remarkable eighteenth-century reservoirs constructed to feed the Canal du Midi – 89 hectares of water surrounded by woods and now used for bathing, sailing and surfboarding, as well as for filling up the canal.

Just to the northeast is Sorèze. Here the Benedictines founded a monastery which took the name of the River Sor. The Protestants destroyed it, but it was rebuilt in the seventeenth century and the Benedictines founded one of the most renowned schools in France here in 1682. Initially it was to take 'the sons of impoverished gentlemen and of army officers who have fallen upon hard times'. In 1758 the Benedictines took the revolutionary step of adding the study of Greek and Latin to the curriculum of maths, geography, history, French and foreign languages – as well as swimming, horse-riding and fencing.

In 1776 Louis XVI transformed this remarkable institution into a military academy. A former Benedictine monk named François Ferlus managed to buy the buildings after the Revolution, in order to preserve what he could of the school's former excellence. Pupils were taught here again from 1813. In 1854 it passed into the hands of the Dominicans, who appointed Père Lacordaire as head, the most famous preacher of his age who wanted (as he said) to

live only with God and children. Lacordaire died in 1861 and is buried in the abbey church.

Today the eighteenth-century buildings of the college at Sorèze lie in a huge park. Sorèze itself is blessed with pretty medieval houses as well as the fortress-like belfry of its sixteenth-century church, and is an excellent centre for excursions and walks in the Black Mountain, with its forests, its patches of verdant pastureland, and its long stretches where nothing grows at all.

The D85 runs directly west to Revel (with many picnic spots on the way) and then to Saint-Félix-Lauragais, worth seeing for its thirteenth-century bastide, its broken-down walls set with houses, and its market square filled with half-timbered buildings. Here the parliament of Toulouse sat in 1482, fleeing the plague. Just outside the village a couple of windmills stand on a Stone Age site.

West of Saint-Félix, look out for the D622 and turn left, following the road through the hilltop village of Vallègue (with its dominating seventeenth-century château and its eighteenth-century church) as far as Villefranche-de-Lauragais, a bastide which Alphonse de Poitiers founded around 1270. In 1355 the English took Villefranche-de-Lauragais and destroyed everything in sight.

The N113 now runs southeast for 22 kilometres back to Castelnaudary, passing the infamous town of Avignonet on the left. In 1242 the Cathar seigneur here murdered the two inquisitors whose remains can be seen in Toulouse cathedral. Leave the world capital of *cassoulet* a second time by crossing the Canal du Midi south and taking the D623 southeast for 17 kilometres to Villasavary. When I was last there the parish priest had died and the church was locked; but I got the key from the shop opposite the restored market hall close by the wine press and enjoyed its arcades and vaults, its classical organ gallery and its renaissance pulpit.

From Villasavary the D119 winds through a few

Will Fanjeaux, the thirteenth-century home of St Dominic, soon fall down from neglect?

kilometres of vast panoramic views up to the walled village of Fanjeaux, with its medieval houses and a fine mid nineteenth-century covered market. Fanjeaux was settled by the Romans and its name itself derives from the temple they built to Jupiter here, Fanum Jovis. This became the country of St Dominic, the monk charged with the impossible task of converting the Cathars by preaching rather than savagery and murder. On the bridge is a remarkable Cathar cross, for by the time Dominic arrived the town had become a centre of Catharism.

Dominic made his home at Fanjeaux in 1206 (his house is still here), and was extraordinarily successful in the village. Two Cathars, it is said, once lay in wait to kill the saint, but could not bring themselves to do so when they saw his holy face. Again, Dominic was debating with some heretics when he asked for a heavenly sign to bolster his arguments. A bolt of fire flashed down and charred a great beam in the debating chamber – a beam still to be seen in the second chapel on the right as you enter the church of Fanjeaux.

Languedoc countryside between Fanjeaux and Fendeille.

This building is worth a visit for other reasons too. The romanesque exterior with its octagonal, two-storeyed tower and seven-arched doorway shelters a strikingly ornate chancel and an entirely successful baroque high altar (restored in 1975). This depicts the assumption of the Virgin Mary, lit naturally from behind, with cherubs in the clouds. A fourteenth-century Madonna in the first chapel on the right is matched by a thirteenth-century Madonna in the second chapel on the left. Here too are a seventeenth-century marble font and a seventeenth-century organ.

Dominic conceived the idea of setting up a community for nine women, all converts from Catharism, who would live in silence, poverty and prayer. The site he chose was Prouille, 3.5 kilometres north of Fanjeaux. Close by lived a group of Dominic's followers – so here began the realization of the three Dominican ideals: houses of prayer, a supply of trained preachers and shelters for the converted.

The nunnery of Saint-Dominique at Prouille was completely destroyed at the Revolution. What could not be destroyed was the Dominican ideal. After Père Lacordaire restored the Dominicans to France in 1843, Madame J. de la Gravière gave them back the land on which the nunnery of Prouille had stood, which she bought back in 1855. Rebuilding began in 1885. You drive to the basilica of Notre-Dame at Prouille along a cool avenue of trees. Today it is still unfinished, but the Dominicans have returned.

Leave the monastery and travel northeast to Bram over the motorway. It is worth taking the D4 to Fresquel from here, simply to see the banks of Riquet's Canal du Midi once more: boats moored, men sitting fishing under the plane trees, and the brilliant locks – apparently simple but in fact a single lock intricately separated by a basin from a double lock, thus enabling the canal to reach the level of the Fresquel aqueduct.

Rejoin the main road (the N113) which runs for 21 kilometres back to Carcassonne, and from there take the road northeast to Conques-sur-Orbiel. Ahead looms the Black Mountain. Only the square keep of the eleventh-century château at Conques still survives. I was once in the place de la Libération here looking on the map for the road to Lastours when a crippled old man chewing a mint leaf hobbled up and asked if he could help. At one point as we talked the mint dropped out of his mouth onto my map, but he courteously took it back with a graceful apology. He told me he was half-crippled as the result of five years in Nazi prison camps, including the Stalag at Hamburg. There, he said, the daily food was sometimes no more than a piece of bread half the length of his fingers. He remembered killing a dog and eating it as though it were a sheep. Whenever a camp guard threw down a cigarette butt, someone picked it up.

This wizened old *maquisard* pointed me north along the D101. As I drove on I passed the village war memorial. Of the thirteen killed, only three fell at the front. Two men deported with my old friend never came back.

Lastours was once dominated by no fewer than four châteaux. This is the country of the powerful gorge de l'Orbiel, and four mighty keeps rise from four rocky peaks left standing by the waters. To reach the châteaux you must climb 800 metres on foot, but the view alone is worth it.

Six kilometres from here (reached by driving a little way back along the D101, turning left into the D111 and left again along the D511) you can visit the grotte du Limousis, a splendidly encrusted set of caverns created by a subterranean river (open daily throughout the year, but with an extended break in the middle of the day).

The route continues east for 5 kilometres to Villeneuve-Minervois, a neat little village whose château was built by Isarn d'Aragon, seigneur of Villeneuve from 1195 to 1236. The fortified romanesque church boasts a classical doorway and a spare gothic interior as well as an eighteenth-century marble pulpit.

The road runs east from Villeneuve-Minervois

The hilltop village of Cabrespine, northeast of Carcassonne, shelters beneath the Black Mountain in the gorge of the River Clamoux.

through undulating countryside, skirting the Black Mountain, to Rieux-Minervois. Pause to look at its byzantine-style romanesque church, built in a heptagonal fashion extremely rare for this region. Lost again I here asked a lady with a bicycle to direct me to the road for Azille. Lost herself she asked in return if I could tell her how to get to the Canal du Midi, where her husband was waiting on a canal-cruiser.

Azille is in fact easily found by taking the D206 east. Its fortified church inside a fortified village boasts another eighteenth-century marble pulpit (a little more elaborate than that at Rieux-Minervois). But what delighted me was the contrast between two war memorials in this village – one secular, the other religious. Inside the church the monument 'Aux Héros d'Azille' depicts a dying soldier of World War I welcomed by a Jesus radiating glory. Outside (in the allées de la République) another memorial 'Aux Glorieux de 1914–1919' portrays a French soldier on guard, with a classical lady holding a victor's palm over his head.

As such names as Villeneuve-Minervois and Rieux-Minervois (plus a good few others: Caunes-Minervois; Laure-Minervois; Peyriac-Minervois) indicate, these are the plains, slopes and scrubland that stretch from the edge of the Cevennes in the south to the upper limit of the département of the Aude, known collectively as Le Minervois. The mediterranean climate, the blue skies and the white chalky soil make it ideally suited for cultivating grapes. Cicero himself praised the wines of this region in Roman times. A battalion of vintners is dug in north of the River Aude, producing red wines based mainly on the Carignan grape (with some Grenache and Cinsault). Red Minervois wines were designated entirely appellation d'origine contrôlée in 1985. Fruity and fresh, with a fine scent, if not necessarily great, they are invariably pleasant and go extremely well with a cassoulet or with game.

In the midst of the Minervois is one of the most extraordinary sights of the whole region: Minerve itself. Drive northeast from Azille through vineyard country to the once fortified village of Pépieux (with its gothic church and the dolmen of Les Fades) and on to Cesseras. The D168 now runs east to Azillanet, where you take the winding D10 north. Superb views, lovely rock formations and dry stone walls that remind you of parts of Yorkshire in England are eclipsed as the road begins to descend round and round into Minerve, the Cathar city which Simon de Montfort took in 1210, burning alive 140 heretics and destroying the stronghold (all that remains is a scarred stone finger defiantly pointing to the sky).

The Templar gateway into Minerve is still called the 'gate of the perfect ones', a reference to the austere leaders of the Cathars. As so frequently happened, a Cathar stronghold later became the home of Huguenots. The Huguenot leader repaired the ramparts and moat of the château in 1582, only to have them destroyed again (by Richelieu) in 1636.

Minerve is as old as the wine of Minervois, if not older. Inside its romanesque church is the earliest surviving altar in Gaul, dated 456. Its stoup, even older, once supported a pagan Roman altar. But it is the site of this city which is most memorable, a deep limestone gorge cleft by the River Brian near its confluence with the Cesse. The Cesse has dug deep tunnels in the rock, creating natural bridges, one 110 metres long, the other a stupendous 250 metres.

In summer the Cesse flows underground, leaving its beautiful chalky bed entirely dried up. Follow its route east by way of La Caunette to Aigues-Vives, a site inhabited in the sixth century before Christ. The village is notable for its fine churches (some ruined, some restored) and delightful old quarters around its château. The D910 (just outside the village on the way from Minerve) leads southwest to Aigne, where impressive Roman villas have been excavated, vying in interest with the twelfth-century church which sports a massive gothic belfry. The same road continues southwest for another 12 kilometres to

At Lastours only four solitary keeps remain from the fortress which Pierre-Roger de Cabaret and his descendants built in the twelfth and thirteenth centuries.

85

Olonzac, where Iron Age man has left a dry stone girdle around a hill settlement, where the medieval fortifications once boasted fifteen towers and two great gates, and where the Huguenots erected a cross south of the town in 1620.

Two kilometres from here you cross the Canal du Midi and join the D610. Turn left and after a short drive east take the D611 which runs south for 10 kilometres to Lézignan-Corbières, a peaceful little town which Protestant troops savagely pillaged during the Wars of Religion, happily failing to destroy the fourteenth-century fortified church of Saint-Félix. The façade of the *maison biscornue* (the 'crooked house') next to the church is a curiosity. Its owner, a stone-mason, has decorated his home with all manner of bizarre and eccentric objects. The town also has a statue to the novelist and poet Joseph Anglade (1868–1930), who was devoted to Languedoc nationalism and the troubadours of his beloved region.

Lézignan-Corbières is understandably devoted to Corbières wine. More entrancing than this particular vintage, in my opinion, is the wine museum here, full of intriguing relics of our bibulous past.

The road southwest from Lézignan-Corbières crosses the motorway and after 16 kilometres reaches the fortified village of Lagrasse, situated where the valleys of the Orbieu and the Alsou meet. Here six hermits founded an abbey on the left bank of the Orbieu shortly after Christianity reached Gaul. The story goes that Charlemagne christened this region 'luxuriant valley' (*vallée grasse*, hence Lagrasse). He certainly granted a charter to the abbey founded in the eighth century by a friend of St Benedict of Aniane named Nimphridus. The mighty early fourteenth-century belfry of the abbey church, though unfinished, rises to 40 metres.

The fifteenth-century houses, narrow streets, and a twelfth-century stone bridge across the Alsou make

A gnarled, nail-studded doorway at Lagrasse.

Lagrasse a picturesque spot, with monastic and priory buildings that are still romantic, even though the monks disappeared at the Revolution. The eighteenth-century abbot's lodgings can only be described as a palace.

From Lagrasse the most enjoyable route back to Carcassonne winds along the gorge of the Alsou. After 20 kilometres it reaches Trèbes, where the delightful aqueduct built by Vauban over the Canal du Midi in 1687 is matched by a little bridge of five arches over the Aude that is partly Roman. And Carcassonne lies a mere 7 kilometres west.

The twelfth-century stone bridge and the fourteenth-century abbey church of Lagrasse.

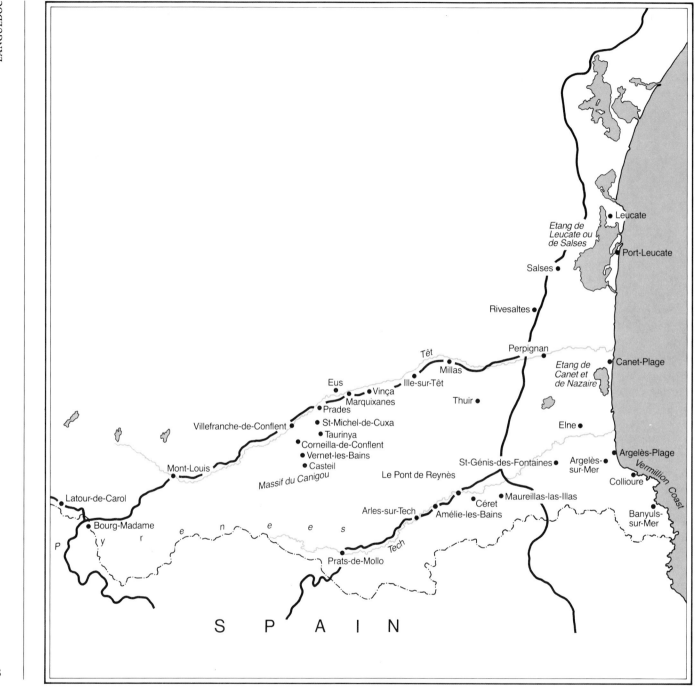

3
Mont Canigou and the Vermillion Coast

Perpignan – Salses – Prades – Villefranche-de-Conflent – Prats-de-Mollo – Amélie-les-Bains – Collioure – Banyuls-sur-Mer – Elne

Long, long ago, legend has it, a farmer named Pynia lived in the tiny hamlet of Cortals, 1750 metres up the slopes of Mont Louis in the Pyrenees. Tiring of his monotonous life on the peaks, he set off to find a more hospitable home, following the torrent of the River Têt as it rushed down between the rocks, driving his two oxen and his primitive plough in front of him. Reaching a green, fertile and well-watered plain not far from the sea, he ploughed a field and built himself a house. Around the field his successors built a wall. The house was the first of many. Pynia had fathered the city that bears his name: 'Père Pynia', Perpignan.

The truth is different, though scarcely less romantic. In the beginning Perpignan was a small Roman town on the right bank of the Têt. The Romans called it Ruscina – from which the whole region, Roussillon, derives its name. They built their fort where the Via Domitiana from Spain to Italy crosses the Têt, in a spot long occupied by vigorous tribes who had traded as far away as Greece. The barbarian invasions ruined their settlement, though today Château Roussillon to the east of Perpignan marks the spot.

In the tenth century 'villa Perpinianum' reappears in history, 5 kilometres upstream of the original Ruscina. In the next century the counts of Roussillon made it their home. The counts were relatives of the counts of Barcelona who became kings of Aragon in

1150; the last Count of Roussillon, Gérard II, left Perpignan to this Spanish branch of the family when he died in 1172.

King Louis IX of France failed to win this territory from Aragon and in 1238 he renounced all claims to Roussillon in favour of King Jaime I of Aragon. Jaime I in his turn left his French territories (which included the Balearic Isles, the Cerdagne between the Têt and the Sègre, and Montpellier, as well as Perpignan and Roussillon) to his younger son, and the future king installed himself at Perpignan.

He took the title King of Majorca. For seventy-eight years, under three kings of Majorca – Jaime I (1276–1311), Sancho (1311–24) and Jaime II (1324–44) – Perpignan flourished culturally, economically and artistically, the envy of the older branch of the royal family. In 1344 King Pedro II of Aragon won the lands back from Jaime II by force of arms at the battle of Lluchmayor.

Perpignan was still coveted by the greedy eyes of the kings of France. Louis XI took the city in 1463 and proved such an intolerable master that the people rose against him ten years later and were brought down only after a terrible siege. Louis ordered his soldiers to drive monks and consuls out of the city – and anyone else who could give him trouble. The French then savagely repressed the citizens until 1493 when

Charles VIII, needing to free himself of domestic troubles in order to pursue his ambitions in Italy, ceded Roussillon once again to the Spanish.

Perpignan was dubbed 'Fidelissime Ville' by the Spaniards, though its citizens frequently chafed under the domination of Madrid. In 1604 the Catalans revolted, proclaiming Louis XIII of France as Count of Barcelona. Two years later the French and their Catalan allies re-occupied Perpignan, welcomed by a starving population.

Nevertheless Perpignan and Roussillon remained technically Spanish until 1659 when, after more than a hundred years of dispute and conflict, they were ceded to the French by the treaty of the Pyrenees. The brilliant military engineer and architect Vauban flung fortified walls round the city; these were demolished only in the 1900s in order to make room for expansion, for Perpignan had begun to flourish economically after the building of a railway station in 1862. This is so dull that Salvador Dali can only have been joking when he described it as the centre of the universe, 'a source of inspiration, a cathedral of illumination'.

A century and a half of French absolutism could not quench the fiery independence of the people of Perpignan. One of the city's greatest sons was Dominique François Jean Arago. The eldest son of François Bonaventure Arago and his wife Marie Roeg, Arago was born in 1786 at Estagel, where his father was a landowner. The whole family moved to Perpignan in 1795 when François Bonaventure became cashier at the mint.

Young François wanted to become a soldier, but while at the École Polytechnique in Paris, where he was head of his class throughout his university career, he discovered an extraordinary talent for astronomy. The profession was by no means a sedentary one. On a geodetic expedition in Spain he was held prisoner and spent some time in gaol in Algeria. When he returned to France in 1809 he was elected to the Institut de France as an astronomer, became professor of descriptive geometry at the École Polytechnique, and also ran the Paris observatory. A warm-hearted, volatile personality, he made close friends (such as the great German scientist Alexander von Humboldt) and violent enemies. And his astronomical theories and discoveries in the fields of magnetism, electricity and light were brilliant.

Tragically he began to go blind. But by now this radical genius had been drawn into politics. After the July Revolution of 1830 in favour of a liberal monarchy he was elected to represent his native *département* and sat in the Chamber of Deputies till a year before his death in 1852. He was an enthusiastic advocate of railways, canals, and the electric telegraph. The distinguished teacher now promoted educational reform, believing that the lower classes should also share the benefits of schools and universities. He passionately defended freedom of association.

The finest months of his political career came after the February Revolution of 1848 abolished the monarchy. As a member of the provisional government he became minister of the navy, then of the army, and finally president of the Executive Committee. In his short, heady tenure Arago managed to outlaw corporal punishment at sea and improve the rations allotted to sailors. He also abolished slavery in the French colonies. In June, however, he found himself at odds with such socialists as Ledru-Rollin and Louis Blanc.

Yet Arago remained a deputy, still passionate for freedom and democracy, and when Louis Napoleon became president in 1852, he refused to take the oath of allegiance. In 1853 he died.

Opposite the classical Palais de Justice (built in 1859) and the elegant tea-shops of Perpignan, François Arago's statue stands in the place Arago, pigeons sleekly resting on his outstretched arm. The mediterranean aspect of Perpignan (and indeed all Roussillon) is here emphasized by the fact that all the trees around place Arago are palm trees. The River Basse (a tributary of the Têt) is flanked with lawns and flowers. In front

The romanesque entrance to the lower chapel in the palace of the kings of Majorca, Perpignan.

The remarkable double chapel of the palace of the kings of Majorca. The lower chapel, dedicated to St Mary Magdalen, was the queen's; the upper chapel, dedicated to the Holy Cross, was the king's.

of Arago's statue a notice points left towards the uniquely bizarre palace of the kings of Majorca.

However you approach Perpignan you cannot miss this greatest legacy of the transient Majorcan rule. Walk or drive from place Arago up the rue Grande-Monnaie with the old city on your left, looking out for directions. Fortified in brick and stone in the sixteenth century (and further defended by Vauban in the next), the palace itself, built for Jaime I, is a massive two-storeyed rectangle around a vast interior courtyard (used these days for distinguished concerts by, for example, the London Symphony Orchestra). From the west entrance you walk up long stepped ramps to the courtyard. Notice the curious use of river pebbles as well as brick in the construction, the graceful loggias,

the double chapel to the east. The south side is taken up entirely by the Salle de Majorca, whose interior boasts huge arches and fireplaces. The chapel surprised me by having gothic tracery *painted* on its blank walls.

If you have the energy, climb to the top of the barbican (which has three rooms and seventy-seven steps) for a panoramic look at the city: from one side you see the *château d'eau* on the left and the Lycée Arago to the right; from the wall opposite the panorama on the left includes the church of Sainte-Marie-de-la-Réal (built in 1320), the chapel of Saint-Dominique (a thirteenth-century abbey church with the remains of its monastery buildings), and the cathedral, while the late medieval church of Saint-Jacques (whose furnishings are rich and precious) can be seen in the distance.

Take rue Jacques I from the palace to return to the old city, joining the rue des Troubadours and turning left at the shady little square (the place des Esplanades) to walk past the church of Sainte-Marie-de-la-Réal. The anti-pope Benedict XIII held a council in this church in 1408.

Place Rigaud sports a poorish statue of another of Perpignan's distinguished sons, the artist Hyacinthe Rigaud. Rigaud was born here in the year Perpignan finally became French. Often considered merely a painter of flattering portraits of the rich, Rigaud's genuine originality has been ignored. Studying in Montpellier, he became fascinated by the works of Anthony van Dyck, on whom he decided to base his own style. At his death he possessed eight Van Dyck's of his own, as well as four paintings by Rubens and – unusually at this period – no fewer than seven by Rembrandt.

He reached Paris in 1681, and was almost immediately given the *prix de Rome* for his painting of Cain building the city of Enoch. In 1688 his portrait of Louis XIV's brother was hailed as magnificent.

The garden entrance to the church of Saint-Jacques, Perpignan.

Thenceforth Rigaud's career as court-painter was assured.

Honours were showered on the portraitist, including a royal pension. He was also a careful man. He took fifty-one years finding a suitable wife (and finally chose the widow of the usher to the King's Grand Council). His accounts survive, meticulously kept and revealing that he charged less if the sitter's head was the only original part of a portrait and if the clothing could be copied from earlier works. Yet the fact that he and his well-paid assistants turned out as many as fifty portraits a year should not blind us to the grandiose baroque – even rococo – skills he brought to his art. Without Rigaud, the influence of Rubens in France might never have decisively overcome the gentler tradition of Poussin.

The Musée Rigaud, in a seventeenth-century palace at No. 16 rue de l'Ange, has the great advantage of not boring the visitor with too many and extensive galleries. It also boasts no fewer than three self-portraits of the artist. The one I like best is called *Rigaud in a turban*. Here too you can see Rigaud's magnificent baroque portrait of Cardinal Bouillon, whose red robes are almost outmatched by the crimson curtain billowing behind him.

North of the place Rigaud is the rue Main-de-Fer. The risqué, slightly macabre façade of the house of the Iron Hand (Maison de la Main-de-Fer), built for a wealthy shipowner in 1509, appears on the left on the way to place Gambetta and the cathedral of Saint-Jean-Baptiste.

As you reach the cathedral, you see what appears to be a nondescript chapel on the south side. Inside is one of the most impressive crucifixions in the whole of France, the *Dévot Christ* as it is called, a gilded corpse, dead of pain and exhaustion, his skin stretched over

Left The decidedly fanciful forged iron belfry of Perpignan cathedral.

Right One of the most harrowing of all medieval crucifixes, the *Dévot Christ* of Perpignan.

his protruding ribs, his head to one side, the mouth open, the eyes closed, the tendons of his arms stretched unbearably, the veins on his crossed legs knotted and protruding, three huge spikes pinning him to the cross.

For many years experts guessed that this masterpiece dated from the early sixteenth century, since it first appeared at Perpignan in 1528. Recently some relics and a document of 1307 were discovered inside the statue, proving conclusively that this is not one of the cruel images of Spanish piety but in fact a product of Rhenish mysticism, a creation of the gothic art that flourished in the early fourteenth century in and around Cologne.

On Good Friday the crucifix of the *Dévot Christ* is taken down and placed on a black catafalque in the cathedral square, for a ceremony which more than anything else illustrates for me how Spanish this part of France can be. The 'Procession of the Sanch' at Perpignan originated six and a half centuries ago, and is still organized by the arch-confraternity of the Sanch, founded in 1416. 'Sanch' is Catalan for blood (*sang* in French) and refers to the precious blood of Christ. Throughout Good Friday afternoon, veiled in long, pointed, red or black hoods and dressed in red or black robes, a file of penitents (known as *caparuxtes*), led by a red-hooded man tolling a bell, walks the streets of the city to remember the passion and agony of Jesus. Some beat muffled drums; others carry statues: the Virgin Mary, crowned, with her robe embroidered with seven swords piercing her heart; Jesus agonizing on the Mount of Olives; a seventeenth-century *Ecce Homo* from the church of Saint-Jacques; a great cross with the instruments of the passion (nails, a hammer, the ladder to take the dead Jesus down from the cross). The whole affair is rendered even more melancholy by the singing of ancient Catalan hymns in honour of the saints, even though these are technically called *goigs* (pronounced 'gotch'), which derives from the Latin *gaudium* meaning 'joy'.

The cathedral of Perpignan itself stems from King Sancho of Majorca's decision in 1324 to replace a building that had stood here since the early eleventh century. The nave is superb, each arch of the vault decorated with geometric patterns, while the magnificent marble high altar, begun in 1618, displays a gilded wooden statue of John the Baptist. He wears a golden hairy coat and his finger points to a gilded Lamb of God. Behind him are the striped red and yellow colours of the Catalans.

I was able to walk up to the high altar with impunity one Sunday after Mass, since three babies were being baptised – not in the font but by the altar. At French baptisms people mill around at will (save for the godparents, who hold candles), taking photographs even during the Lord's Prayer. So I wandered up to the holy of holies to marvel at the exquisite carving of the reredos. The portrayal of the Last Supper is especially taking, with *fourteen* participants where you expect only thirteen: Christ, the twelve apostles, and a serving lad crouched down by the table filling up the wine.

Perpignan cathedral has other splendidly carved altars, the most flamboyant that of St Peter (with a slender Jesus suffering flagellation), the most homely that of the Virgin Mary, with a sturdy St Joseph, his basket over his shoulder, striding ahead of Mary, her son and a donkey *en route* for Egypt. This particular altar was carved at Barcelona shortly before 1700 by the baroque master Onuphre Lazare Tremullas. And another lovely reredos is that known as the *Mangrana* (which means pomegranate), dating from the early sixteenth century and depicting scenes from the life of the Virgin Mary.

The treasures of Perpignan cathedral are by no means exhausted by these works. Go under the organ (with a huge carved head suspended from its case) to see the rich collection of relics kept there: bits of St Eulalia, St Julian and St Victor, some in fine reliquaries. (You can illuminate this dark chapel by putting a coin in a slot to the right as you go in.) Seek out the tombs and statues throughout the cathedral, as well as the eleventh-century font with its Catalan inscription: 'The water from the sacred fountain stifles the hissing of the guilty serpent.' And notice the shutters of the organ case, painted in 1504 with scenes of the baptism of Jesus and the feast of Herod. Whoever was responsible has crammed these pictures with delightful oddities, such as a crane standing on one leg in the River Jordan where the baptism is taking place.

The cathedral belfry at the west end is topped by a graceful iron cage. This was forged in 1743 to hold a bell which has struck the hours at Perpignan since 1413.

Leave the cathedral by the west door into place Gambetta, once the parade ground of Perpignan and now surrounded by pink brick houses of the early sixteenth century as well as the maison Villalonge of 1660, where Louis XIV once stayed. The narrow rue Saint-Jean runs west from here to one of the most magical parts of the city of Perpignan: the place de la Loge.

The Loge de Mer was built as the city stock exchange and a court for settling maritime disputes in the late fourteenth century. It was exquisitely enlarged in the sixteenth. It is best appreciated over a coffee at one of the tables opposite, from where the earlier parts can be clearly distinguished from the later, which extend flamboyantly to the west. At the corner – a symbol of Perpignan's sea trade – is a weathercock in the shape of a galleon.

Further down the street is the town hall, begun in the fourteenth century, with seventeenth-century wrought-iron gates protecting its courtyard, followed by the fifteenth-century Palais de la Députation. The town hall is embellished with three bronze coats of arms, belonging to the three orders who were once represented there, the *haute bourgeoisie*, the middle class, and small merchants and farmers.

Quite as entrancing as these delightful buildings is the black statue of a graceful, slightly chubby Venus who stands at the entrance to the place de la Loge. She was created by Aritide Maillol in 1928. Maillol was born at Banyuls-sur-Mer in 1861 and died there in 1944. His first creative work took the form of paintings and tapestries inspired by the group of decorative artists who called themselves the Nabis. When almost forty, he began to lose his sight, the result, it is said, of

the strain caused by working in tapestry. He decided to become a sculptor. Almost invariably he created monumental nude women, always recognizably his own, though with a pedigree going back to classical Greece. You can see a much earlier nude than Maillol's Venus, representing the spirit of the Mediterranean, a few metres away in the courtyard of the town hall. This time the bronze nude pensively supports her head with her left hand, her elbow on her knee; but she is indisputably by the same hand as the Venus. Critics have wondered how Maillol got away with calling virtually the same nude by different titles, but I can gaze at his nudes for a very long time without tiring. His crouching bronze naked lady in the Musée Rigaud (called *Monument to Debussy*) is to my mind a sufficient reason in itself for a visit.

Summer meals in the open air in the place de la Loge are inevitably pricier than in the villages of the Languedoc (though not desperately so), but the ambience and the food are worth it. Catalan cuisine is as old as any in France, as medieval cookery books testify. One reason is the proximity of the sea. Another is the abundant game on the mountains. A third is the great variety of terrain, so that different fruits and vegetables are always at hand at the various seasons. A fourth gastronomical blessing comes from the richly stocked rivers and streams. (I have read that trout breed in 900 kilometres of water in Pyrénées Orientales.)

At the Grand Café de la Loge you can feast on *escargots à la catalane*, snails garnished with ham, onion, peppers and parsley. This is a dish often served with garlic mayonnaise (aïoli). Made of olive oil, egg yolks, lemon juice, salt and garlic, this is a magical concoction that the locals often stir in their soup.

The Café de la Loge will make you traditional dishes from some of the medieval Catalan cookbooks if you are there at the right time of the year. From February to April you can order *turbot aux asperges de la Salange*, a recipe deriving from the thirteenth-century manual of Sent Sovi, the fish piquantly done with asparagus and almonds. At any time of the year you can order *le canard aux fruits*, a duck stuffed according to the fifteenth-century recipe of Mestre Robert in his *Libre del Coch*, but you have to order it two days before.

While I should be the last to declare that Côtes du Roussillon conjures up visions of truly great wines, wherever or whatever you eat, the wine should be Roussillon, a name virtually synonymous with the *département* of Pyrénées Orientales. The sun shines in Roussillon for an average of 325 days a year. Grains of vine pollen have been found in the prehistoric caves of Tautavel northwest of Perpignan, which means that men and women have been washing down their food with Roussillon wine for at least 250,000 years. Today Côtes du Roussillon is an *appellation d'origine contrôlée* wine known chiefly in its red variety. But there is a white version, made from the Maccabeo grape, and also a fruity rosé that is a perfect accompaniment to *charcuterie*, and therefore much drunk by myself on picnics. Côtes du Roussillon Villages refers to a *cave co-opérative* based on twenty-five communes between the rivers Têt and Agly west of Perpignan, known for making gentle reds.

Another reason for drinking Côtes du Roussillon in Perpignan is that you are subsidizing good music. A Camargue farmer named François Pagès and the wine *co-opératives* together sponsor the annual Perpignan music festival in July and August. I have heard the choir of Radio-France here and been pleased at my own little contribution to the profits that have subsidized it (though I would not quite emulate the superlatives of the festival's president that 'at the end of this twentieth century, marked by a consumer society which is difficult, egotistical, polluted, materialistic, there remains in the heart of each of us this need for infinity, universality, generosity, capable of prompting a farmer from the Camargue and the Roussillon vintners to engender such effervescence. . .').

After lunch walk north from the place de la Loge along rue Louis-Blanc to see the Castillet, a fortified gateway made of brick in 1367 and enlarged in 1479 as a kind of watchtower over the whole city. For a long time the Castillet served as the city gaol, though today it more fittingly houses a museum of Catalan culture and history.

Five kilometres east of Perpignan on the way to the Mediterranean you pass Château Roussillon, with its ruined romanesque church, its twelfth-century tower and its excavated Roman forum, the original Ruscina. After another 8 kilometres you reach the sea, and in particular the seaside resort of Canet-Plage, a vast expanse of fine golden sand, on exactly the same latitude as Rome and deformed with countless undistinguished holiday homes and hotels. To the south is the 1000-hectare lake of Canet and Saint-Nazaire, now classified as a protected nature reserve and peopled with pink flamingoes.

To the north is Port-Leucate, the oldest bathing resort on the littoral. The road from Canet-Plage is lined with holiday resorts on either side of you all the way, their pretentious names ('Palm Beach', 'Le Lido', 'Little Venice', 'Le Club House') matching their insipid architecture. Yet there is good swimming here, as well as surfboarding and yachting, especially at the lake of Leucate, which soon appears on the left. The sea is extensively farmed for mussels, which are a cherished delicacy in this part of the Languedoc.

Port-Leucate offers an instructive example of an outmoded architectural fad. When the doctrinaire functionalism of Le Corbusier was considered avant-garde, one of his closest collaborators, George Candilis, was commissioned to develop this town. Eschewing the traditional patterns of Catalan architecture, Candilis produced such cubic monstrosities that a new architect, Michel Duplay, was commissioned to re-humanize it all.

At Leucate-Plage you turn left to reach the village of Leucate itself, dominated by its ruined old fortress and a great deal more alluring. In 1590 a local girl named Françoise de Cézelly rallied the villagers to defend their fortress against the Spaniards, and her statue is now in the place de la République.

Drive on from Leucate to join the N9 which runs south to the magnificent château at Salses. As you

---

A tributary of the River Têt tumbles over the rocks.

reach the town, you are greeted by the ruins of an earlier château that was built by King Alfonse II of Aragon in 1172. In 1497 Ferdinand of Spain decided it was not strong enough for modern warfare, especially since Charles VII's French soldiers had started using metal cannon balls and had destroyed a lot of it. Ferdinand instructed the military architect Ramiro to construct the present massive building at Salses, whose lower walls are some 12 metres thick and whose upper walls are designed to make the cannon-balls ricochet back on the enemy. I find the sheer size of the château overwhelming, with room for no fewer than 1000 soldiers and 300 horses.

Sixteen kilometres south of Salses is Rivesaltes, worth visiting for at least three reasons: first for its sweet Muscat, a reviving aperitif; secondly, to look inside its mid seventeenth-century parish church, if only for a glimpse of the profusion of ecclesiastical treasures which it contains; and thirdly to see the old houses, above all the one in which Marshal Joffre, the hero of the Marne, was born on 12 January 1852.

Sculpted by Maillard, Joseph Jacques Césaire Joffre sits martially on his horse at the end of a great line of plane trees at Rivesaltes. Joffre was made commander in chief of the French armies in 1914 only because his superiors were politically unacceptable. The French had been forced back almost to Paris when Joffre ordered a counter-offensive on 6 September 1914, so ruining the Kaiser's plans to win a speedy victory.

As Joffre later wrote, 'The best and greatest portion of the German army was on our soil, with its battle-line jutting out a mere five days march from the heart of France. This situation made it clear to every Frenchman that our task consisted of defeating this enemy and driving him out of our land.' Unfortunately Joffre did not achieve his last ambition, as his armies were unable to break through the German lines. Joffre also failed to foresee the need to provide fortifications for Verdun, which was attacked by the Germans in 1916. But he fell from power chiefly because of his political opponents in Paris. In December 1916 he was offered the position of Marshal of France, a title which had been obsolete since 1870, and he was effectively retired. He died in 1931. Had he lived another nine years what, I wonder, would he have thought of the fact that several thousand French Jews were imprisoned in the town of his birth in 1940, before being deported to Hitler's Germany?

I once drove the 25 kilometres southwest from Rivesaltes to Millas (along the D614) on the second Thursday in August, not realizing that the town's annual festival (Feria in Catalan) was about to begin, but knowing that I had a room at the one *auberge* in the place. I ate well, and especially enjoyed the fish soup. In the Languedoc this is almost invariably served with a *rouille* sauce made of garlic, roasted red peppers and bread, pounded together and then liquidized with a little fish broth. Then I went to bed. The annual festival began at 11 pm and continued till 4 am, with music, dancing and much laughter. I experienced little difficulty noting the time since the church clock at Millas chimes every quarter as well as the hours, followed a minute or so later by the chimes of another clock on the market hall.

The Feria continued till the following Sunday and included the hair-raising spectacle of bulls chasing people in the streets. Miss Feria (chosen the previous Sunday) presided over everything, including a *super concours* of *pétanque*, the French equivalent of bowls. Apart from such excitements, Millas is a charming town, with some of its fortifications still intact, the ruins of a royal fortress (Força-Real) to the north, and the fifteenth-century church of Saint-Eulalie, with its battlemented tower (probably to stop visitors smashing the clock). Inside are a massive double font (one set inside the other), and a superb eighteenth-century reredos by Tremullas, depicting St Sebastian.

My host at the *auberge* called the bull by its Spanish-Catalan name: *toro*. I was reminded of a report made by one of the royal supervisors in 1652: 'The people of Roussillon call and esteem themselves Catalan, and consider it an insult or an injury to be called French or Catalan-French.' Maybe they have come to see themselves as Catalan-French by now. Certainly the signposts in this part of France are in both French and Catalan, as, for example, Ille-sur-Têt and Illa de Tet.

From Millas I drove southwest through Ille-sur-Têt and the foothills of the Massif du Canigou, the earth scorched by the sun at that time of the year but with enormous peaches on sale everywhere. The evening before my host had served a fillet of sole with peaches that was to me quite unusual and totally satisfying.

After half an hour or so you come to an enormous long reservoir and it is worth turning left into Vinça at this point, which King Jaime of Aragon fortified in 1245. Here the houses are made of stones that look like great pebbles and the information office is in an arcaded house dated 1616. Vinça has five fountains, and at one men and women were washing their clothes with great slabs of carbolic soap.

The door of the church is studded with fine ironwork, and over it you can make out the faded inscription, '*Liberté, Egalité, Fraternité, 1789, République Française*', as if no-one has bothered giving it a second coat of paint since the Revolution. The baroque furnishings inside the gothic church are so splendid that you almost miss the fine, spare, grey-brown stone vaulting. In the south transept is the chapel of the Holy Sacrament, with a retable by the Carcassonne sculptor Jean-Jacques Melair, carved in 1734 (the year when the church was consecrated). In all the convoluted splendour don't miss the carving of a naked faun dancing amongst grapes. An earlier retable by Joseph Sunyer in the chapel of the Rosary shows St Teresa of Avila in a place of honour just below the Trinity. In the bottom left-hand corner an angel makes sure Joseph, Mary and the baby do not get lost on their way to Egypt.

Return to the main road and drive on southwest for a couple of kilometres to Marquixanes, another lovely half-fortified village, dominated by the Dormidou peak which towers over it. The whole village rises up to the church, in a square called the plaça de l'Església. (The street to the presbytery is called Carreró de la Rectoria.) Walk up to the church through the arch. The church tower, dated 1611, has four narrow pepperpot towers. Nothing prepares you for what is inside: an extraordinary collection of baroque retables, brought here for safety from other churches in the region.

Take time to walk down the narrow streets of Marquixanes, enjoying the smell of delicious Catalan cooking. Then drive 3.5 kilometres west along the D35b to one of the most delightful villages in Roussillon – Eus, fortified, perched on the mountainside, its church (dating from the eleventh century) ruling over everything like a fortress. Inside the wall the houses climb on top of each other up the mountainside. As you drive up, the broken walls of the château appear behind the church. I do not know why this village needs two churches, but there is a second one, dating from the eighteenth century.

Depending on your youth and agility, park the car and climb up to explore this village, so unspoilt that it seems peopled with spirits of the past. You can also eat at one of two restaurants. I have tried *L'Escabèche*, which means 'Green Lizard'. Simply reading the menu made my mouth water. Starters included anchovies from Collioure (*anchois de Collioure*); grilled mullet (*rougets grillés*); another fish dish, with glazed grapes (*gambas aux raisins glazés au Banyuls*); and what I chose, *Pa amb oli*, which the waitress explained was grilled bread with mountain ham, tomatoes and onions. That was followed by liver with lardons and grapes, cooked with Muscat (*foie à la Rouste aux raisins et Muscat*), and the meal ended with a species of sorbet with wine called *granité au vin de Collioure*.

The D35b continues towards Prades (transforming itself into the D35 *en route*). This is where the famous Spanish cellist Pablo Casals established himself, after refusing to live in his own country while it was governed by the fascist dictator Franco. No doubt it was a sacrifice to leave Spain, though I should think the difference was not all that great. A bust of Casals (1876–1973) can be seen as you go into Prades. An annual music festival, which he founded in 1950, keeps his memory fresh. In the centre of the town stands an apparently simple church with a twelfth-century tower whose interior is a riot of Spanish baroque carving. St Peter blesses us from behind the high altar, attired in a splendid papal tiara, another masterpiece of the sculptor Sunyer. There is no longer any stained glass in these churches, for the chief

This bronze cherub stands outside the church of Saint-Pierre, Prades.

problem is to keep out the heat, not to let in light.

Prades' excellent market takes place on Wednesday mornings in the place Arago and neighbouring streets. And four times a year – on the first Tuesdays of Lent, June and September and on 20 December – people flock in from the neighbouring cantons and villages for the Prades fair. The restaurants serve countless grilled mussels (which the French would call *moules grillés* but Catalans call *la moulade*) and *la cargolade,* a dish cooked on vine shoots and consisting of little grilled snails, sausages, bread with aïoli, and lamb chops.

Leave Prades south by the D27, following the signs for the abbey of Saint-Michel-de-Cuxa. Dating from the mid ninth century, it lies in a magical setting at the foot of the Massif du Canigou (which rises to 2785 metres). The Prades music festival takes place here. Among the abbey's monks was the celebrated St Romuald, who founded other monasteries and his own

monastic order. Pierre Orselo, Doge of Venice, retired to Saint-Michel-de-Cuxa and left the monks his fortune when he died in 987.

Having inspired artists, the religious, peasants and rulers for a millennium, it seems scarcely credible that this exquisite abbey should have been left to be vandalized after the Revolution, yet much was pulled down and sold. Fortunately the cloisters are a still beautiful (if truncated) reminder of the abbey's greater past, and some of the remaining twelfth-century capitals are fantastic. Others were taken away in the nineteenth century, and you must visit a museum near New York in the valley of the Hudson if you want to see them.

The Benedictines have now returned to this extraordinary and huge monastery, with its monumental tower. (Another one collapsed in a frightful storm during the winter of 1838.) And the interior of the church today is both stark and peaceful.

The abbey of Saint-Michel-de-Cuxa opens for a couple of hours in the morning and afternoon, but if you arrive at the wrong time there are plenty of excellent picnic spots nearby, though the iron mines at Taurinya have turned the water of the nearby stream a browny ochre. If you drive further along the winding road there are stupendous views after Taurinya, especially of the torrent of Saint-Vincent (which dries up to become a chalk bed in summer).

The road winds down to the spa called Vernet-les-Bains, which legend relates was founded by a group of Tuscans following Hercules through this part of France. Certainly this has been a thermal station since the Middle Ages, but it fell on bad times as a result of the Thirty Years War. Business picked up again in the eighteenth century and especially in the late nineteenth, when the baths became fashionable among wealthy English people. (Rudyard Kipling loved to take the waters here.) Today the place has all the

The abbey of Saint-Michel-de-Cuxa, for centuries a power-house of Christian spirituality in the West.

traditional accoutrements of a spa, including a casino. Old Vernet also boasts some historic houses, as well as its ruined château.

If you want to see inside the church of Saint-Saturnin at Vernet-les-Bains (and there are a few interesting pieces of church furniture, including fifteenth-century stalls), it is only possible to do so on certain afternoons. The church is closed at other times, save for Sunday services. I put a bottle of Côtes du Roussillon Blanc de Blancs to cool in the fountain (it is easy to hide one) while visiting the church, and then sat in the shade in the square sipping a glass, watching men, women and children play *pétanque* and studying the war memorial. This is specifically dedicated to the *Entente Cordiale* between Britain and France and consists of two stern figures of indeterminate sex, sitting side by side and not quite holding hands, the one carrying a sword, the other a trident.

Monks have the habit of building their monasteries in inaccessible places, and if you wish to visit the abbey of Saint-Martin-du-Canigou, 2 kilometres south of Vernet-les-Bains, you must be prepared to park your car at the hamlet of Casteil and endure an uphill walk of about thirty minutes. It is well worth the effort. The Benedictines built a double church at the beginning of the eleventh century, transforming the first one into the crypt of the second, the whole monastery set on a rocky, triangular promontory 1093 metres up the Massif.

There is no road over the mountain, but for those who like walking there are well-marked paths along the ridge. If you are car-bound drive north, by way of the village of Corneilla-de-Conflent – Corneilla derives from a Roman villa called Corneiliana – where the counts of Cerdagne had a winter residence and founded a canonry for Augustinian monks as well as a splendid parish church. Beyond Corneilla-de-Conflent the road joins the N116 at Villefranche-de-Conflent, a town that has scarcely changed since the Middle Ages.

The spa of Vernet-les-Bains, still prized for its thermal waters.

Count Guillaume-Ramon of Cerdagne founded Villefranche in 1092, but only twenty-five years later it was inherited by the counts of Barcelona. Its walls were built in the eleventh century and strengthened in the fifteenth, when it belonged first to Castile and then to Spain. Subsequently the French took the town, and Vauban strengthened the walls yet again. Under Louis XVI in 1783 a couple of monumental gateways were added, one facing France, the other facing Spain. And yet mercifully no-one sought to ruin the ancient streets, with their romanesque and gothic houses. The church of Saint-Jacques, featuring pink marble doorways made by the masons of Saint-Michel-de-Cuxa, remains a fine example of twelfth-century unpretentiousness (though, as we have come to expect, its interior is another rich treasury of religious art).

Three hundred metres before you reach Villefranche-de-Conflent is the entrance to one of the better subterranean caves of the region: the Grotte des Grandes Canalettes, with a guided tour that takes an hour and seems to be on offer all the year round.

The N116 now runs southwest towards Andorra, reaching Mont-Louis after 29 kilometres. The Louis involved is Louis XIV, who ordered Vauban to construct a citadel here at the confluence of the Têt, the Aude and the Sègre. Built between 1681 and 1691, Mont-Louis stands 1600 metres above sea-level. The town ramparts and defensive ditches remain as the great military engineer left them and even the church is dedicated to Saint-Louis. General Dagobert died here fighting the Spaniards in 1793 (his statue is within the walls) and the first commercial use of solar heat was successfully developed here in 1953.

Twenty-two kilometres further on, Bourg-Madame lies on the Spanish border. The village was called Hix till 1815, when the Duke of Angoulême changed its name to flatter his duchess. After so much conflict the frontier is peaceful enough now, but I like to remember those stirring tales of World War II when escapees were smuggled across the border – 'smuggled' being the correct word, since their guides were usually smugglers whose livelihood in peacetime as well as war involved cocking a snook at the authorities. The best

day for the crossing was Sunday, when French and Spaniards would chatter away in Catalan for hours at the border-crossing. The easiest spot to cross was at Latour-de-Carol, about 3 kilometres northwest of Bourg-Madame. Escapees would travel there by train, dressed as locals, and – desperately trying to appear nonchalant – stroll across the border with their smugglers.

It is easier to cross today. To return to France by a quite spectacular drive, turn left for Ripoll. The Spaniards have notices telling you how high you are climbing – 1100. . . 1200. . . 1600 metres above sea-level. The road is flanked by a great cliff on the right, but happily it is edged by a barrier. Ripoll, 40 kilometres away, boasts a superb romanesque cathedral, with a marble doorway protected by a glass porch; a memorial to both sides in the Spanish Civil War; and a Saturday market in the plaça Gran, selling baskets, leather and earthenware. (Once, lying in a little late in the hotel on the square, I was knocked up by a friendly policeman, who pointed out that my car was parked exactly where someone had the right to sell handbags; but he kindly found me another parking spot, and I went back to sleep.) But since this book is about France and not Spain, drive on by way of the D151 along the Ter valley through Camprodón to Molló and then cross the border to climb down the mountainside and reach Prats-de-Mollo (which has plenty of good hotels). The drive from Ripoll should take about 45 minutes, though in all it is only 35 kilometres.

The stunning Spanish countryside continues into France, with the brown, green and white colours of the eastern Pyrenees ahead. Although Prats-de-Mollo was rebuilt as a bastide by the King of Majorca in the early fourteenth century, it comes as no surprise that the French refortified it in the seventeenth. (The ubiquitous Vauban was here in 1683, building a fortress north of the city.) In any case, its earlier

ramparts fell down during an earthquake in 1428. The town is an important centre for hiking and excursions into the magnificent surrounding countryside – although the local Syndicat d'Initiative insists that simply staying there will improve the health of those with chronic respiratory problems.

A delightful twisting road runs beside the river to Arles-sur-Tech, with deeply cleft gorges to left and right. Small tunnels dig through the rocks. At one point a great bridge crosses the Tech. Sometimes there are stark rock faces, contrasting with gentle green wooded slopes swooping down to the water. When the river-bed is dried up the scene is even more spectacularly, with masses of granite rocks piled fantastically on top of each other.

Anyone visiting Arles-sur-Tech will want to see its monastery founded in the late eighth century that was ruined by the Normans and rebuilt in two stages. Part was consecrated in 1046, the rest in 1157. Oddly enough, the church faces east, not west. The oldest treasure of the abbey, protected by a grill on the left side of the sombre great church, is a fifth-century sarcophagus with the relics of its patron saints Abdon and Sennen. Year in, year out this sarcophagus is said to fill mysteriously with some 600 litres of holy water. In former times tiny amounts of this liquid were distributed to visiting pilgrims. One drop cured the cancerous face of Guillaume Gaucelme de Taillet, who died in 1204 and is buried here, commemorated by a fine romanesque statue.

Quite apart from such edifying tales, the abbey is well worth visiting for its entrancing gothic cloister with white marble arcades supported on slender stone columns (you reach it through the church), the fourteenth-century chapter house and rare frescoes of 1157.

Another curious feature of the ecclesiastical architecture of Arles-sur-Tech is the romanesque-gothic church of Saint-Sauveur, which was sold to a M. Noëll-Ladeaux for 260 francs in 1807. Twenty other persons bought it from him so as to stop him demolishing the building; it remains private property to this day.

Sunlit roses and a shady street at Villefranche-de-Conflent.

Left Fortified Prats-de-Mollo, guarding the pass over the Pyrenees into Spain.

Above The winding arched way up to the church at Prats-de-Mollo.

Northeast from here is another town that decided to change its name in the nineteenth century to please a fine lady – this time the queen herself. Amélie-les-Bains-Palalda was known simply as Bains-d'Arles till 1840, when Amélie, wife of Louis-Philippe, came to take the cure.

The waters had been curing people long before her time. The Romans called the spot 'Aquae Caldae' ('hot waters') and cherished its thermal properties. The remains of their own baths are incorporated in the modern institution – which also happens to be called the Roman baths (*les thermes romains*).

You reach the Roman baths by turning right off the main street into the insignificant-looking rue des Thermes. Here sauna, steam and mud baths serve not only cripples with pathetically wasted limbs but also the healthy planning to become even healthier. The Palm Tree Hotel flourishes next door, and Amélie-les-Bains looks sleek and profitable. No less a personage than Hyacinthe Rigaud painted the reredos behind the high altar of the church of Notre-Dame-de-Montalba. Since 1942, Amélie-les-Bains has been organizing an international folklore festival, with celebrated groups of dancers coming from as far away as Bulgaria, Bolivia, Hungary, Israel, Paraguay, Antigua, Greece and Turkey, as well as from Spain.

Perhaps a hint of a less sophisticated past creeps into Amélie-les-Bains when you reach the open-air public wash-house to the south of the town, with strings of wire to dry the clothes. The architecture also betrays signs of less elegant times. Vauban has been at work here and you can see his hospital for old soldiers, crippled in the service of the State.

Follow the road northeast to Le Pont-de-Reynès and a couple of kilometres further turn right along the D618 into the village of Céret. Céret was here long before Hannibal and his elephants passed this way. Traces of the old Roman bridge across the Tech can still be discerned, replaced in 1321 by the narrow 'bridge

A corner of Arles-sur-Tech. Note the contrast between the uncut stones of the far wall and the smoother later ones in the foreground.

of the devil', with an arch 45 metres long and a height over the water of 31 metres.

Céret became a city in the ninth century and was fortified in the fourteenth, with one gate pointing towards Spain and the other towards France. It seems fitting that the final peace between the two countries was negotiated in the Capuchin convent here. Look out for the eighteenth-century church with its thirteenth-century belfry and a lovely fourteenth-century white marble porch.

Then Céret rested on its laurels until the twentieth century, when a group of artists led by Pablo Picasso and including Braque, Matisse, Marc Chagall, André Derain, Dufy and Juan Gris began gathering here. Céret witnessed the birth of Cubism. The city fathers were enlightened enough to commission Maillol to design their war memorial after World War I, and he created an unforgettable image of a woman weeping for her dead sons in the place de la Liberté. After all this I was disappointed with the museum of modern art, hoping for too much from what is a worthy little collection.

One sport that attracted Picasso here was bullfighting. The arena at Céret is not a classical amphitheatre, but a bullfighting ring, constructed in 1960. Here you can see a plaque to José Falcon, killed by the bull Culchareto on 11 August 1974, aged thirty-three. Less bloodthirsty is the festival of traditional Sardane dancing held in the arena every August. Whenever the writer Aragon watched the Sardane (so he tells us), he felt an inexplicable warmth in his veins, his heart was on fire and he knew why the sky was blue.

Céret has a good open-air swimming-pool, and it was so hot at the time of the Sardane festival when I attended it that I needed no further stimulus to feel on fire and preferred to join the children, watched over by their grannies, in the water. The neighbourhood abounds with camp-sites, many with their own swimming-pools, especially on the road east (the D618) to Maureillas-las-Illas (which is flanked with vineyards producing Rivesaltes). Maureillas-las-Illas has a square dedicated to the bullfighters of the world. The British are not included.

Above The thirteenth-century towers of château de Palalda still protect Amélie-les-Bains, a spa known as Bains-d'Arles until Queen Amélie of France took the waters there in 1840.

Right Boats moored at Collioure in front of the old lighthouse, which also serves as the church tower.

The Phoenicians and the Romans also fished along the Vermillion Coast.

Since non-campers cannot use the camp-site pools, I recommend a visit to the seaside from here. Argelès-sur-Mer lies a mere 22 kilometres east, under the motorway and by way of Saint-Génis-des-Fontaines. In 1986 some of the vineyards along this route were no more than blackened twigs as a result of forest fires. Saint-Génis-des-Fontaines has a fine pre-romanesque church, with a lintel over the doorway which is justly renowned as one of the earliest attempts at monumental sculpture in the West. The inscription says it was done in the twenty-fourth year of the reign of King Robert the Pious, i.e. 1020. Yet there should be much more here. The church was once part of a

Benedictine abbey founded in 819. Incredibly, when the monastery was dissolved in 1924, *copies* of the capitals and marble columns of the cloister were made by local sculptors and the originals were sold off. Two of the arcades are today in the Louvre; parts of the monastery are in Philadelphia in the United States; another part has been erected at the château of Mesnuls in Île-de-France.

On the way to Argelès-sur-Mer watch for the signs to Collioure and turn right along the N114. So you reach the Mediterranean, with pine trees and sandy beaches and all the paraphernalia of the tourist industry almost blinding you to the charms of the ancient fortified town, where the peace treaty beween the King of Aragon and the King of Majorca was signed in 1298. Even the Dominican church has become a wine shop.

The road runs south, with the vineyards of the excellent sweet white wine known as Banyuls Muscat climbing away inland. Collioure appears, set on a charming bay, with a lighthouse acting as belfry for its seventeenth-century church, a sturdily fortified castle, yachts in the harbour and at sea, little coves with anchored boats and people sitting on the rocks with the water splashing gently. Small wonder Derain, Picasso, Dufy, Matisse and the rest loved the place. And people have been trading from here with the Greeks for 2500 years.

Nine kilometres south of Argelès-sur-Mer is Banyuls (Banyuls-sur-Mer in French; Banyuls de la Marenda in Catalan). In season the pebble beach is packed as well as the sands, the harbour is crammed with boats, pseudo wine caves invite you to sip and buy the wine, restaurants offer the justly famous Banyuls anchovies. The sculptor Maillol was born and died here, and his grave bears one of his own statues. Here too Maillol created another sad war memorial, not one of his monumental nudes but a dying soldier and two mourners.

I like to drive south, just outside the town, up to a parking place that is usually deserted. This is a fine spot to sample a glass of Muscat, while you look out over the whole bay: the blue sea; yachts; people fishing; the pebble beach in the distance; the rising vineyards. What you cannot see from here is the sub-aquatic exploration much favoured at Banyuls and fostered by the marine institute dedicated to François Arago (the Laboratorie Arago), with its fascinating aquarium.

Drive back to Argelès-sur-Mer, turning right there to reach Argelès-Plage at the other end of the Vermillion Coast, invariably crowded to bursting point in summer with swimmers, surf-boarders and sunbathers. To find quieter spots to bathe, drive north along the D81 and turn inland for Elne.

Historically and architecturally the ancient city of Elne sums up much of this extraordinary region. Hannibal camped outside its walls on his way to Rome in 218 BC. In the early fourth century AD the town's fortunes revived under the Emperor Constantine, who named it after his mother the Empress Helena (hence 'Elne'). In 350 one of Constantine's sons was murdered here. The Visigoths made it the seat of a bishop around 570. When the Moors threatened Elne the Franks fought them off, and Charlemagne made the city capital of the seven counties he created in this part of the Languedoc.

In the lower city a new cathedral was built in the ninth century. Not two centuries later prosperity led the bishops to build a bigger one, in the upper city. The citizens threw up the city walls in 1157, walls that served them well under siege from Philippe the Bold in 1255, the King of Aragon in 1344, Louis XI in 1474 and Marshal Turenne in 1641.

The bishops did not move to Perpignan till 1602, after which Elne continued to prosper, as it does today, the garden centre of this succulent part of France.

Signposts take you round the ramparts to the former cathedral – one tower brick, one stone; one romanesque, the other nineteenth-century (the arches so flat that you think it should tumble down). Only two buttresses hold up its apse. Walk round to the cloisters. In contrast to the sorely mutilated examples seen elsewhere, those at Elne are perfect. They are also very fine – the richest in sculpture still existing in this part of France, as Viollet-le-Duc observed half a century before some of the others in the Languedoc were crazily dismantled.

The cloisters at Elne were in fact once at risk, long ago, for they were partly vandalized in 1285. The monks rebuilt them, re-using the old stone and marble. Since they were built over two centuries, their capitals and details range from twelfth-century romanesque to fourteenth-century gothic. The oldest part is the south wing, abutting onto the cathedral.

Eleanor Elsner, a British visitor who reached Elne quite by chance over sixty years ago, found a sleepy old town whose old sandstone houses seemed to be crumbling away. But once she reached the cathedral cloisters, she was enchanted. They were, she judged, perhaps the most beautiful in Europe. Her description is perfect:

'The columns are of white marble, each in a different design and most richly decorated. Some are fluted, some twisted, some carved like the trunk of a pine tree, and others covered with the most wonderful carving of foliage and figures, the design of which seems to have been miraculously preserved. Every single column is worth long and separate study, but it is the colour of the marble that makes this old cloister so entrancing. Since the twelfth century it has stood bathed and soaked in sun, and its colour has become a mellow creaminess which sometimes brightens to a soft rose, and sometimes deepens into a real yellow.'

Eleanor Elsner thought the cathedral itself of little interest. She was wrong. This fortified basilica may be spare inside, but it houses no fewer than five medieval altars, and a couple of fourteenth-century tombs, one of which, that of Bishop Raymond de Costa who died in 1310, stands in a gothic chapel which he had built himself. There is a fourteenth-century retable dedicated to St Michael the Archangel. And the font, decorated with acanthus leaves, may even be Roman.

Since Elne is both the centre of luscious gardens and also close by the sea, why not sample one of the regional specialities that matches fish with fruit here, say anchovies and black olives, cooked in puff pastry (*feuilleté aux anchois*)? If that sounds too exotic (though I do not think it is), what about baked oysters (*huitres aux four*), garnished with grated cheese, a chopped

Above **An exquisite entombment of Christ in the cathedral at Elne.**

Left **Rich romanesque sculpture in the cloisters of the former cathedral of Elne.**

onion and breadcrumbs? And then drive west for 20 kilometres along the D612 to the delightful town of Thuir, to stock up at the renowned wine cellars of Byrrh, which devotees justly dub one of the cathedrals of wine. Here you can marvel at the largest oak vat in the world, capable of holding a million litres of wine. And armed with a few of the reds, rosés or whites of the Aspre vineyards of this area, you are scarcely 10 kilometres southwest of Perpignan.

St-Bauzille-de-Putois

Nîmes

St-Martin-de-Londres

Hérault

St-Guilhem-
le-Désert

Viols-le-Fort

Lodève

Puéchabon

St-Jean-de-Fos

Canal du Rhône

Salagou

Lake
Salagou

St-Félix-
de-Lodez

Aniane

Octon

Gignac

Camargue

St-André-de-Sangonis

Mourèze

Salasc

Clermont-l'Hérault

Montpellier

Petit

Villeneuvette

Lattes

Paulhan

Maguelone

Nizas

Caux

Montagnac

Balaruc

Frontignan

Pézenas

Bouzigues

Mèze

Bassin de Thau

Sète

Orb

Béziers

Canal du Midi

Vias

Marseillan-Plage

Agde

Le Cap d'Agde

Aude

M e d i t e r r a n e a n

Narbonne

Sigean

4
Royal Cities and High Monastic Places

Montpellier – Sète – Agde – Béziers – Narbonne –
Pézenas – the lake of Salagou – Saint-Guilhem-le-
Désert – the Grotte des Demoiselles – Aniane

When I first visited Montpellier, I thought for a moment I was in Vienna, that city of cafés serving creamy coffee while pianists play Franz Lehar on grand pianos. The Café du Doyen was advertising a 'café-concert' at 10.30 that evening, and I made a note of this and went, only to find myself invited to '*rock avec les Crazy Cats*'.

Many seemed to be enjoying this experience. I can only record that it was my one disappointment with the city on that occasion. Perhaps I gave up too soon, leaving for a drink elsewhere. Another 'café-concert' was advertised at the Café du Doyen for an evening later in the month, this time inviting visitors to enjoy '*rock tolousain avec les Boys Scout*'. If the spirit of Toulouse can imbue a Boy Scouts' band (could it have been such?), perhaps the Crazy Cats would have seemed less crazy as the evening wore on.

A previous visitor to the city, Rabbi Benjamin de Tudele, had a quite different experience. Visiting the Jewish community at Montpellier in the twelfth century, he was amazed at its prosperity. 'This is a spot perfectly situated for commerce,' he noted, 'and traders both Christian and Saracen, Arabs from the Gharb, merchants of Lombardy and from the great kingdom of Rome, from every part of Egypt, Greece, Gaul, Spain, Genoa and Pisa crowd its streets.'

There are disadvantages in being rich. Although trade brought wealth to Montpellier, this was coveted by overweening nobles. Trade also brought disease. The great epidemic of 1348 reached the town by way of the trade route from the Indies. The Duke of Anjou, governing Montpellier on the king's behalf, seemed heedless that the population had been decimated by the disease. His solution to the problem of raising the same amount of revenue from fewer people was to increase taxation. The methods used by his tax farmers became increasingly savage. In 1379 he imposed a new tax of 12 francs on every hearth and provoked an insurrection.

On the night of 25 October five of the Duke's officials and perhaps eighty royal commissars, sent to collect new subsidies, were massacred. The people, by now almost starving, are said to have eaten their very bodies. Reprisal was swift. The revolt had no coherent organization, and soon its leaders were at Anjou's feet.

In *A Distant Mirror* Barbara Tuchman has described the Duke's sadistically staged return to Montpellier:

'A vast procession of citizens over the age of fourteen was led through the city gate. . . , along with surviving officials, ecclesiastics, monks, faculty and students of the university. Lined up on both sides of the road, they fell on their knees crying "Mercy!" as the Duke and his men in armour rode by. Along the way were stationed magistrates in gowns of office without mantles, hats, or belts, women in unadorned dress, citizens with halters round their necks, and, finally, all the children under fourteen, each group falling to its knees in turn to cry ''Mercy!'' '

Then the Duke condemned six hundred to death: a third by hanging, a third by burning and a third by beheading. Everyone else was to forfeit half their goods.

It was grim play-acting. Nearly all the sentences were withdrawn the next morning. In fact very soon afterwards King Charles V thought it wiser to put the administration of Montpellier in other hands – hands unfortunately quite as rapacious as Anjou's.

Compared with many other cities and settlements in the Languedoc, the history of Montpellier is comparatively short. It was founded in the ninth century by refugees from the town of Maguelone on the coast, which had been savagely attacked first by the Saracens and then by the northern King Charles Martel. They chose their spot well, for until the creation of the port of Sète in the seventeenth century their new city, with access to Lattes on the coast, was the principal French Mediterranean port. It lay on an important salt road, as well as on one of the pilgrimage routes to Santiago de Compostela. One of Montpellier's churches is called Notre-Dame-des-Tables because money-changers and bankers set up their tables around it to cope with the needs of medieval travellers.

Montpellier gained market rights in the twelfth century, as well as the right to be governed by democratically elected consuls. This independence and prosperity was soon reflected in the construction of fortifications. In this secure and prosperous environment a celebrated medical school was established, followed by other faculties. Petrarch learned law here, Nostradamus and Rabelais medicine.

The city was by no means always French. In 1208 Montpellier was the birthplace of Jaime I of Aragon, but later in the same century the city paid allegiance to the kingdom of Majorca and the future Jaime I of Majorca was born here in 1248. Then, in 1349, King Jaime III of Majorca sold this birthplace of kings to Philippe de Valois of France for 120,000 gold crowns. The nearby township of Montpelliéret already belonged to the French, and so the two were united as one town.

Shortly before the insurrection of 1379 the Languedoc Pope Urban V founded a Benedictine monastery at Montpellier whose abbey church became the cathedral in 1536, when the bishops of Maguelone transferred their see here. Soon the city began to prosper again. In 1432 Jacques Coeur, the brilliant merchant and treasurer to Charles VII, made Montpellier one of his principal trading centres. A century later the treasurers of France were permanently based here.

I have been describing the history of a basically medieval and renaissance city. Why, then, are so many of the churches of Montpellier post-Reformation? The answer lies in a remarkable religious transformation: within twenty-three years of the establishment of the Catholic bishopric, Montpellier had turned Protestant. The conversion was initiated in the 1530s, by men who came initially from Germany by way of the River Rhône. Lying low at first, they emerged into the open with savage *éclat* in 1559, not only here but wherever they felt strong enough to profane sanctuaries and destroy 'superstition'. The conversion of many of Montpellier's citizens to the tenets of the Reformation radically affected the look of the city, since the Protestants proceeded to pull down most of the Catholic churches and convents. The greatest loss was the thirteenth-century abbey of Saint-Benedict, built by Pope Urban V, which was almost totally destroyed.

Soon Montpellier was taking a leading role in the Federation of Reformed Cities, basking in the toleration which Henri IV offered Protestants in the Edict of Nantes of 1598. The university here was still universally admired. The town's prosperity, dented by the religious transformation, now returned.

Tranquillity did not last. Louis XIII besieged this armed Huguenot stronghold in 1622 and took eight months to overcome its defences. The citizens, capitulating, cried 'Long live the king, and have mercy on us!' Richelieu built a royal citadel here, and when the Protestants showed signs of reasserting themselves, dismantled the city walls.

Yet in spite of everything Protestantism continued to flourish at Montpellier, as did the wealthy bourgeoisie. Even when Louis XIV abandoned religious toleration in 1685, Montpellier remained a haven for the Huguenots of France.

Louis XIV, who repealed the Edict of Nantes, had in fact inherited an economic crisis in the Languedoc and his minister Colbert vigorously set about creating new wealth. The Canal du Midi was constructed; new industries were founded. And Montpellier profited.

Protestant or not, in 1672 Montpellier became the chief city of the Languedoc (and still claims to be its beating heart). The city lost its principal position at the Revolution, but the coming of the railways and the development of the wine trade brought further prosperity. Until 1853 the only railways in the region were those linking Montpellier with Sète and Nîmes.

The wine trade proved a mixed blessing. In 1876 a third of Montpellier's vines were destroyed by phylloxera. Replanted, the vineyards went in for colossal overproduction, with little regard to quality. As a result, when Algerian wine began to be imported in the early twentieth century, there was a tremendous crisis here (and virtually throughout the Midi).

Only in recent years has the crisis been overcome – and Montpellier has suddenly come alive again economically. Happily, the city authorities have taken care not to allow the ill-effects of industrial expansion to touch the entrancing centre of the old city.

I like to compare my own experience of a foreign town with those of the classic tourists of the past, so the first time I visited Montpellier I sat in a café by the place de la Comédie, read the relevant part of Henry James's *Little Tour in France* and looked up my notes of what others had said about it. Oddly enough, they don't agree about whether Montpellier *is* a beautiful city. That cunning Henry James tries to have it both ways, judging that the place has neither the gaiety of a modern town nor the solemnity of an ancient one, and concluding that 'it is agreeable as certain women are agreeable who are neither beautiful nor clever'.

A hundred years earlier Arthur Young was also equivocal. 'Montpellier, with the air rather of a great capital than of a provincial town, covers a hill that swells proudly to the view; but on entering it you experience a disappointment from narrow, ill-built, crooked streets, but full of people, apparently alive with business,' he wrote. Yet he conceded that the aqueduct of Montpellier was magnificent: 'a very noble work'.

Young had also imbibed the fashionable medical view that the air of Montpellier was bad for foreigners, and he records that most British people were moving to Narbonne for that reason. Thirty years earlier the novelist Laurence Sterne suffered similar qualms; indeed, his doctors told him that it would be fatal if he stayed any longer at Montpellier. (Sterne asked: 'Why, good people, were you not kind enough to tell me this earlier?')

Henry Matthews, writing as a self-conscious invalid in 1820, reported that he liked Montpellier less the more he stayed there, while the novelist Stendhal considered it one of the ugliest cities he had ever seen. And yet the philosopher John Locke once declared he would rather go twice to Montpellier than to anywhere else.

I personally have no doubts: Montpellier to my mind is charming. Old Montpellier is small enough to walk round and varied enough to make you linger. Steeped in the classicism of the eighteenth century, Arthur Young naturally appreciated the classical aspects of the city; we, more eclectic in our tastes today, regard what to him were ill-built, crooked streets as charming medieval nooks and crannies. In the 1st canton (or quarter) especially, narrow winding streets lead to squares and fountains, and you can often see an arch straining to keep a couple of leaning buildings apart.

Happily, too, the old city of Montpellier has evaded all attempts to introduce the ugliness of the twentieth century. It exhibits a mixture of many styles and faces, but they are all seductive. And more than any other city in the Languedoc, Montepellier is blessed with gardens. I like it very much.

The square I sat in is an ideal place to begin judging Montpellier's quality for yourself. The place de la

Comédie is enormous. The locals call this massive space the Egg (*l'Oeuf*), because of its more or less oval shape. Making an egg (*faire l'oeuf*) in Montpellier means simply strolling in the square here, sheltering under its parasols, drinking coffee in its cafés. The citizens of Montpellier have been doing this since 1755, when the Egg was laid out on the site of their old city parade ground.

One end is dominated by the enormous theatre of 1888, the mightiest of the late nineteenth-century buildings which flank the place de la Comédie. A theatre has stood here since 1755, but the old one kept burning down. After the fire of 1881, the Parisian architect Cassien-Bernard was hired to create the present ornate building, especially enticing when it is illuminated at night from inside its three mighty arches. I have seen some excellent ballet here.

At the far end of the Egg is a modern shopping centre that deserves a better word than 'complex', since – in spite of its undistinguished architecture – it does work, its bookshops, boutiques and stores airy and accessible, the railway passing strangely overhead.

Montpellier has preserved a tradition of fine fountains. In the centre of the Egg, three Graces were sculpted in white Carrara marble by Étienne d'Antoine in 1776, Graces immodest enough to have been discreetly dressed in living memory, when processions of the faithful passed by. Immodesty triumphed in 1895 when the statue was brought out from the shade of the theatre to the very centre of the Egg.

A long modern fountain and weir created in 1986 to humanize the entrance to the shopping complex matches Étienne d'Antoine's masterpiece in its own way. To the left of the complex is a lovely esplanade, three lines of magnificent plane trees some 500 metres long. Apparently this was a dumping ground for rubble left after the siege of 1622. The city fathers

continually produced abortive plans to beautify the site, but nothing was done until the provincial governor of the Languedoc, the Duke of Roquelaure, took the work in hand in 1723. In my own French garden I have planted trees in a thin scattering of earth over rubble, and then watched them scorch and die. Roquelaure brought young oaks from Lyon, planted them, and he too watched them die. Only in 1774 was water piped here, two little reservoirs created and chestnuts planted. The locals instantly began to bathe in the new pools, until forbidden to do so by an ordinance of 1780, which described their behaviour as 'indecent'.

The present plane trees, far more suited to this climate, replaced the chestnuts in the twentieth century. To the right is one of Montpellier's fine gardens. At the north end is the memorial to the dead of two world wars, at the south end a memorial to the fallen *maquisards* of World War II.

If you walk back into the Egg and go left past the theatre, down rue Victor-Hugo, you will reach one of the two remnants of the city walls, the Babote tower, its lower section built in the twelfth century, its upper section dating from the eighteenth. Astronomers mounted telescopes on the tower after the Revolution; from 1832 an extra section was used for telegraphing messages optically. You can sit in a café opposite and marvel at the thought of the brave idiots who leapt off it in the early years of this century, testing primitive parachutes.

Walk round the tower and as far as the Grand'Rue Jean-Moulin, which returns towards the centre of the old city. Montpellier boasts many handsome seventeenth- and eighteenth-century town houses, and the Hôtel Saint-Côme (No. 32 on the left-hand side of this street) is one of the finest. In his will Louis XV's surgeon commissioned the architect Jean-Antoine Giral to build it as an anatomical amphitheatre where budding medics could watch autopsies and operations. Today it is Montpellier's chamber of commerce.

The rue Jacques-Coeur leads off the Grand'Rue Jean-Moulin, passing under one of the archways that add a charm to the old streets of the city. The former

Louis XV's surgeon Lapeyronie and the biologist Barthez, sculpted by Gumery in 1864, sit outside the medical school at Montpellier.

university chapel of the faculty of arts is on the right-hand side and place Jean-Jaurès at the end of the street houses a market every morning. No. 7 rue Jacques-Coeur is an elegant seventeenth-century town house with a statue of the brilliant financier in the courtyard.

Jacques Coeur, with a fortune based on silks and oils and perfumes, was responsible for building one of the masterpieces of renaissance architecture in Montpellier, the Hôtel of the Treasurers of France (No. 5, in nearby rue Trésoriers-de-France). This superb town house, begun in 1432, was sold to the state treasurers in 1675. They set about embellishing an already beautiful building. A gothic gateway with ogival arcades leads into the courtyard where you find yourself in front of an imposing façade of two superimposed classical colonnades. A magnificent staircase boasts a painting by Jean de Tray representing Justice discovering Truth. And don't miss the emblems of the Sun King, Louis XIV, on the second storey, as well as his motto *Nec pluribus impar* ('Not unequal among many').

Rue Trésoriers-de-France is a medieval street glittering with classical town houses, testimony to the wealth accrued by this great trading city. No. 4 is the Hôtel de Rodez de Benavent, built in the seventeenth century and rebuilt by Giral in 1730, with a splendid staircase, and decorated bays and balustrades; No. 15 is the eighteenth-century Hôtel de Ginestous, whose unpretentious façade belies its sumptuous courtyard (with a painting on the staircase of Pedro II of Aragon reconciled with his wife Marie de Montpellier in 1207).

At the north corner of place Jean-Jaurès, No. 10 rue de l'Argenterie is the former palace of the kings of Aragon. The doorway actually dates from their era (a rare survival in Montpellier), with gothic arches separated by finely sculpted motifs. The arches rise from columns that have dented wagons and carriages over the centuries, and taken some punishment themselves. The kings of Aragon took the palace from a Cathar, Raymond de Mourèze, in the thirteenth century. (Some of the orthodox obviously had a vested interest in the success of the Albigensian crusade.) It abuts onto the palace of the kings of Majorca.

You reach the cathedral of Saint-Pierre, Montpellier, by walking north from the place Jean-Jaurès. Do not trust the advertised opening hours. If my experience is anything to go by, there is no sense in arriving before the afternoon, when the grumpy custodian arrives and unlocks the door.

You can fill in time by exploring a street to the west, which rises alongside the medical faculty of the University of Montpellier. Medicine has been taught continuously in the city for longer than anywhere else in the world, certainly since the twelfth century. Whether it has always been taught well is another matter. As late as 1574 the doctors were still teaching by question and answer, in the manner of medieval schooling:

Question: To cure dysentery, is it better to vomit or be purged?
Answer: To be purged.
Question: How can elephantiasis be cured?
Answer: By castration.
Question: Which is better for a person's health, wine or water?
Answer: Water.
Question: Are men hotter than women?
Answer: Yes.

Some of the ancient disciplines have, alas, disappeared – such as a thirteenth-century course devoted to the properties of alcohol. Did medicine improve with their disappearance? Jean-Jacques Rousseau would have thought not. He came here in 1737 to consult the doctors and complained that 'none of them understood my case, treating me as a mere hypochondriac'.

The medical school was transferred to this noble seventeenth-century building (formerly the episcopal palace) at the Revolution. Giral created its monumental façade. The pompous statues outside are by Gumery, done in 1864 and representing Louis XV's surgeon Lapeyronie and the biologist Barthez.

Inside is a macabre anatomical museum and the Musée Atger, with its unrivalled collection of medical books and drawings. In the courtyard are vestiges of the former Benedictine abbey.

Turning from the scientific to the spiritual, it is

The bizarre baldacchino at the west end of Montpellier cathedral, on which the coats of arms of King Charles V and Pope Urban V can still be traced.

worth retracing your steps to the cathedral. Its west façade is extraordinary, a vast baldacchino with twin turrets sheltering the doorway. This is virtually all that remains of the church consecrated by Pope Urban V on St Valentine's Day, 1367. The rest has suffered enormously over the centuries. Protestants despoiled it in 1561 and again in 1567. Richelieu ordered its rebuilding in 1630. Monsignor Bosquet demolished the gothic choir and replaced it with a classical one in 1773. In 1778 Jean-François l'Épine built the present mighty organ case. Stendhal's verdict in 1838 was that he found the whole cathedral 'ridiculous'.

With the Revolution the cathedral at Montpellier was transformed first into a Temple of Reason and then into a military depot. Napoleon's concordat with the Vatican in 1801 ended this humiliation. In 1843 Pope Pius XI declared the great church to be a 'minor basilica' – apparently a notable honour. In 1857, inspired by this signal recognition, the bishops commissioned the architect Revoil to build neo-gothic transepts and a neo-gothic choir, extending the interior of the cathedral to a length of 95 metres.

There are modern works of art in the cathedral of Saint-Pierre, including altars done in the 1980s by Philippe Koeppelin. The most touching memorial is that to Cardinal de Cabrières, which the sculptor Jean Magrou exhibited at the Paris salon before bringing it here. A bas-relief depicts that extraordinary moment in 1907 when 500,000 desperate vintners descended on Montpellier from as far away as the eastern Pyrenees. Soldiers killed a few of them, but the people of Montpellier took their side. The cardinal himself welcomed them into his cathedral, and there many of these desperately impoverished people spent the night.

In a shady garden behind the cathedral stands the romanesque-gothic tower of the pines (*la tour des pins*) – so-called because of the pine trees that used to grow from the top – the second survivor of the old ramparts. Its last military rôle was to protect beleaguered Catholics against Huguenot mobs in 1562. Subsequently it became a prison and then a reformatory.

Nostradamus prophesied that Montpellier would perish if the pine trees ever died. In 1827, since their roots were threatening the tower's very existence, the municipal authorities ignored the prophecy and dug them up, replacing the pines with less dangerous cypresses. (Cypresses have shorter roots.) A plaque on the wall commemorates Jaime, king of Aragon and Majorca, lord of the city from 1213 to 1276. The inscription is in the *langue d'oc* and reads: 'To him who took three kingdoms from the Saracens [Majorca, Valencia and Murcie], gave just laws to his people, defended the weak, helped the workers, out of love for Saint Louis and Queen Margerita renounced the rights of his inheritance over much of the Languedoc and Provence, and died at Valencia on 26 July 1276.' This fanciful view of a medieval monarch was penned in 1887.

Left The statue of the Sun King, in the promenade du Peyrou, Montpellier.

Above Cupid controls a lion at the entrance to the promenade du Peyrou.

Also in the garden is a monument to the Languedoc historian and archaeologist Albert Fabre (1845–1919). Another member of the Fabre family, François-Xavier, greatly enriched Montpellier, even though Henry James cruelly mocked this 'little, pursy, fat-faced' artist. James discovered that François-Xavier had successfully pursued the Countess of Albany, widow of James Stuart, pretender to the English throne, who was already romantically attached to the playwright Vittorio Alfieri. 'Surely no woman ever was associated sentimentally with three figures more diverse,' James commented: 'a disqualified sovereign, an Italian dramatist, and a bad French painter.'

François-Xavier Fabre, a pupil of David, had gone to Italy and in fact won the *grand prix du Rome* in 1787 when he was only twenty-one. Since he did not approve of the French Revolution, he stayed in Italy for thirty-seven years, picking up not only the Countess of Albany but also a splendid collection of Italian art, which he left to his native city. This was only the beginning of the remarkable collection to be seen today in the Musée Fabre (No. 13 rue Montpelliéret), for in 1846 a rich banker's son named Alfred Bruyas began collecting and commissioning for the museum. His patronage of artists of the calibre of Delacroix and Courbet is what makes the paintings in the Musée Fabre outstanding.

He had a further quirk: he insisted that everyone he patronized should paint him. One result was Courbet's celebrated painting *Bonjour Monsieur Courbet*, which depicts an extremely handsome Courbet being welcomed outside Montpellier by Bruyas and his servant. (Both take off their hats, in respect to the artist, who is about to take Bruyas' money.)

There are seventeen portraits of the melancholy hypochondriac Bruyas in the Musée Fabre; the one by Delacroix enormously impressed Van Gogh, who came here with Gauguin in 1888. As he told his brother Théo, 'it portrays a bearded man with red hair who strikingly resembles you and me, and it reminded me of de Musset's lines, ''wherever I went, an unhappy man dressed in black came and sat beside me, looking on me like a brother''.'

The painting I like best in the gallery is Courbet's famous bathers (*Les Baigneuses*) of 1853, women so ripe and fat that some suggested that the artist had taken a brood mare as his model.

Across the road from *la tour des pins* is a botanical garden whose roots go back to the fourteenth century. Then, in 1593, Henri IV commissioned the physician and botanist Richer de Belleval to create a royal garden for him here. The siege of 1622 ruined it, but De Belleval patiently replanted. An orangery was added in 1802, and the botanical institute of Montpellier was established here in 1889. The scientific garden is today one of the most important in Europe, with some 3000 species set out according to the classification worked out by the botanist August Candole in 1810. But the chief pleasure of the garden comes from simply wandering along its huge alleyways of exotic trees, savouring its lake, its 'English' garden and its plants, and identifying its statues (especially Gargantua, Pantagruel and the rest, who besport themselves around the statue of their creator, Rabelais).

In this paradise I was enormously tempted to sin by taking a plant or two. But then, I thought, would I want people stealing from *my* garden? 'Still', I said to myself, 'I always give a cutting to anyone who asks for one.' Then I remembered that the penalty for stealing is expulsion from the garden.

Another attractive spot for a stroll is Le Peyrou, the heights from which the royal artillery bombarded Montpellier in 1622. In 1688 a pupil of the architect Mansart created a splendid promenade here, a vast rectangle with rounded corners, enriched with shrubs, lawns and trees. An Arc de Triomphe was erected between here and the city three years later. Montpellier still lacked a sufficient water supply, and between 1753 and 1756 the engineer Henri Pitot constructed a double-arcaded aqueduct, 800 metres long and with all the grace of the eighteenth century, bringing the waters of the spring of Saint-Clément from the west to Le Peyrou. The Montpellier architect Jean-Antoine Giral completed the work by designing an exquisite water-tower, the *château d'eau*, at the end of the aqueduct.

Jean-Antoine Giral designed the graceful eighteenth-century water-tower at Montpellier.

The Arc de Triomphe was erected in honour of the triumphs of the Sun King, Louis XIV. It is inscribed 'Louis the Great, having been king for seventy-two years [he reigned from 1643 to 1715], separated, conquered or reconciled people conspiring to fight war lasting forty years, after which peace at last reigned on land and sea.' As a further piece of glorification, Mansart designed a magnificent bronze equestrian statue of the king. In 1717 it was shipped from Paris to Le Havre, from Le Havre to Bordeaux, and thence by way of the Garonne and the Canal du Midi to Montpellier, to be placed in the middle of Le Peyrou. In 1792 the Revolutionaries pulled down this symbol of despotism, and it was melted for the cannons of the national guard. After the restoration of the monarchy it was decided to commission the much smaller statue that stands in its place today.

Leave Montpellier by way of the N112 to drive southwest to Sète. On the way I recommend that you buy a bottle of the excellent Muscat they make at Frontignan, which will undoubtedly come in handy for a picnic.

This little port of Sète, climbing from the sea up the slopes of Mont Saint-Clair, with its lighthouse and picturesque harbour, was called Cette until 1927. The town is a creation of Colbert, situated where Pierre-Paul Riquet's Canal du Midi reaches the sea. We even know the exact date when its first stone was laid: 22 July 1666. Louis XIV helped it to prosper in its infancy by remitting taxes. The French connection with Algeria, the coming of the railways and the construction of larger docks made Sète France's fifth largest port in the nineteenth century.

In consequence it also has a sad and beautiful sailors' cemetery. A notice by the Jean Vilar theatre points you up the path to the *cimitière marin*. I drove there and was welcomed by a sparkling lady with merry eyes – surprisingly merry in view of the fact that she is custodian of this melancholy spot.

But then, the people of Sète regard their cemetery more with pride than sorrow. The poet Paul Valéry was born on 30 October 1871 in a house on the quay facing the port, and wrote a long meditative poem on

Left On the Arc de Triomphe, Montpellier, the megalomaniac Louis XIV is represented as Hercules crushing both the English lion and the Austrian eagle.

Above In the sailors' cemetery at Sète the academician Charles le Maresquier is sculpted lamenting his own death.

the sailors' cemetery. 'I was born in one of the places where I should like to have been born,' he declared, 'where my first impressions came from the sea and from the bustle of a seaport.' Although he spent much of his life elsewhere, he retained the sturdy independence of fishing people. In 1939 he broadcast that the enemies of France were the enemies of free thought. Inevitably the Nazis banned his lectures at the Collège de France in Paris, but they could not quench the old man's spirit. Stopped on the steps of the college by a Nazi with the brusque question, 'What is taught in this place?', Valéry replied, 'This college is a place where speech is free.'

He died on 20 July 1945, having seen the Nazis driven out of France, and chose to be buried in the cemetery at Sète. The jolly custodian of the sailors' cemetery took me to see his tomb, sixth on the right up a narrow path. The grave belonged to his mother's family (the Famille Grassi). On it are lines from his poem on the sailors' cemetery, welcoming the chance to gaze on the face of the deities, having meditated about them for so long.

Actually I prefer the tomb of someone far less eminent than Valéry, the academician Charles le Maresquier (a few graves lower down than Valéry's). He lived from 1870 to 1972 and he is portrayed here with his head in his hands, looking extremely put out to be dead.

The custodian wanted to show me other graves, and I was glad I followed her. Here lies Eugène Herber, born at Sète (or Cette, as his monument has it) in 1878, who died defending the French legation at Peking in 1900. Here, almost opposite Le Maresquier, is the monument to two harbour pilots who were drowned on 6 January 1876 trying to save an American ship.

My sprightly informant explained that the wreaths on the graves are not made of flowers but of stone or metal, because flowers in honour of these brave sailors have already been thrown into the sea. Twinklingly she pointed to niches set in a wall, informing me that since the graveyard is full they have to dig up the skeletons after fifteen years of decomposition and stick them into the cavities, to make room for more drowned sailors. Obviously notables like Le Maresquier and Valéry get better treatment.

A notice on the gate informs the visitor that Georges Brassens is not buried here, but in the cemetery at Le Py (in the direction of La-Corniche-Montpellier, 3 kilometres away). When I asked the custodian why Brassens was not here, she informed me that this was the cemetery for the rich (apart from drowned sailors). Brassens was in the cemetery of the poor.

Did he die poor then, this *boulevardier* and anarchist, whose ballads (especially *Chez Jean*, written for the wife of the man who sheltered him when he escaped from Germany in World War II) I so much loved when the old charmer sang them on television, nearing the end of his life? Not so, said the custodian, but Brassens' family was poor. (He was born at Sète in a family of masons in 1921.) His tomb is *their* tomb (Famille Brassens-Dagrosa). She remembered his funeral in 1981, adding 'as did everyone in Sète, and indeed in France'. It had been conducted by an old friend of this man who feared no-one, a priest – though at Brassens' request he dressed in mufti.

The nearby Valéry museum (with entry free one day a week) now has a section devoted to Brassens. And in the garden is Brassens' first boat, the little *Sauve qui peut*.

You have a choice of route from Sète to Agde, depending whether you want to swim or eat oysters. The oyster route takes you back north through Balaruc and then round the western side of the vast lake of Thau. This is the largest inland lake of the lower Languedoc, with a perimeter of 55 kilometres. It is a natural oyster and mussel factory, with the superstructures of specially created oyster-beds covering the sea for kilometres. At Bouzigues is a museum of 'conchyculture', with much useful information on the breeding and culture of mussels and oysters.

Mèze, 18 kilometres northwest of Sète, boasts a medieval gateway and a fifteenth-century gothic church, but its chief allure consists of countless outlets for oysters. Buy them in shops, and from stalls by the roadside – a paradise for lovers of shellfish. Stuffed squid is another speciality here, the skin tightly stretched round all manner of spicy meats.

From Mèze the D51 runs southwest to Agde. As for my alternative route, if you have renounced gluttony in favour of swimming, leave Sète southwest along the coast by way of the N112. Marseillan-Plage, *en route*, has a lovely beach. Indeed the whole coast road offers sand mercifully free of tourists even in August, and this is where I like to picnic, after a swim.

Agde is on the River Hérault and the Canal du Midi, and is therefore filled with fishing boats, canal-cruisers and fishermen. If Sète is a comparatively modern town, Agde is ancient, founded by the Phoenicians six centuries before the birth of Jesus. A statue of the Greek goddess Agathe (otherwise known as *la belle Agathoise*, and sculpted by Auguste Baussan in the late nineteenth century) looks out over the waters from the main promenade. Left from the goddess, up the rue Honoré-Murat, you will come to the blackish-grey walls of the former cathedral of Saint-Etienne, dating from as far back as the twelfth century. In my view it is not very beautiful, but extraordinary in being made out of lava. In spite of its fine pulpit, I find it remarkable chiefly for its bizarreness. Close by, in the place Molière, a charming gothic church with huge chandeliers, everything well restored in 1979, now serves as a little art gallery.

Walk on past the town hall, built in 1651 and again constructed out of lava. The sight of a black classical doorway is undoubtedly odd. Further on, the rue aux Herbes leads into the pedestrianized old town. On the left the rue de l'Amour climbs amidst outdoor stalls, bookshops, boutiques selling jewellery and art, fish and vegetable shops, cafés and restaurants, the interiors of the old houses often dominated by massive beams.

Here I tried *calamars farcis*, stuffed squid, and liked them very much. At the top of the street I came across a huge fresh fish with a mighty tail, lying on a slab, half-covered with a damp cloth. I asked the fishmonger what it was. To my surprise she answered, 'tuna fish'. I always thought tuna fish were tiny.

Walk back a little way to the street on the left that is also crammed with open stalls – selling paella, pizza, cakes, mussels, sweetmeats, perfumes, clothes, scented soaps and more tuna. The street leads to place Gambetta (containing a sixteenth-century church with a bizarre lava porch and façade), from where you can make your way down to the quay for a boat trip along the Canal du Midi or out to the lake of Thau. Or you can visit the nearby Cap d'Agde, France's premier naturist resort, where there is also a museum of Mediterranean history. Take your pick.

On the way to Béziers from here it is worth pausing at Vias to see the fine fourteenth-century church, also made of black lava. Savaged by Goths, Franks, Vandals, Saracens and above all the Christian Simon de Montfort, Béziers continually rose from its ashes. As you approach, the cathedral dominates the town, rising majestically like a castle above the wide River Orb. Crossing the thirteenth-century bridge, you can drive round the walls up to this strangely turreted ensemble.

The sixteenth-century cloisters are fairly tumble-down and eerie, but they lead to very fine bishops' gardens. Inside the strangely truncated cathedral is a baroque high altar of 1758 and a pulpit from half a century later. Climb up to the renaissance organ gallery to have a close look at the mighty instrument created by G. Ponchet in 1623. Then walk round the outside of the east end for a panorama of vineyards, the river and distant hills.

Béziers has many other lovely churches. It also boasts a Corrida in August lasting five days, and I once went there to see it. I knew that the bulls were let loose to run around the allées Paul-Riquet. This is always a lively square, with its market and the gracious classical municipal theatre at one end, but the theatre was scarcely accessible on the day of the Corrida. The market was still alive, but all round the *allées* barriers had been erected, with men, women and children crowding against them, standing on boxes and seats, to get a glimpse of the coming spectacle. Somewhere a band played bullfighting music. Girls clashed tambourines.

Then there was a sudden silence. The crowd roared as four black bulls, baubles at the ends of their horns,

Above Boats wait by the quay at Agde; tourists can take a trip from here along the Canal du Midi or to the lake of Thau.

Right The strange cathedral of Saint-Nazaire at Béziers, high above the city and the thirteenth-century bridge spanning the River Orb.

were let loose from cattle trucks at the end of the street. Snorting, saliva dripping from their mouths and nostrils, these beasts were harassed and provoked by firecrackers to run along the street, while would-be toreadors waited till the beasts were safely past before rushing out to make a momentary grab for one of the bulls' tails. The spectacle of animals so basely tormented was not pleasant, and I no longer feel excited at the sight of the huge crowd outside the arena at Béziers, waiting for the real bullfighting to begin.

From Béziers the N9 runs 27 kilometres south to Narbonne, to me a fascinating city, ancient and yet seemingly unfinished. The cathedral of Saint-Just has no nave, yet it is an awe-inspiring piece of gothic architecture, built between 1272 and 1340 with delightful flying buttresses, disintegrating gargoyles and flamboyant windows filled with thirteenth- and fourteenth-century stained glass. The ruined west end is almost frightening. It is worth climbing the 256 steps to the top of its north tower, 71 metres high, for a panoramic view of the vineyards round about, although the last time I was in Béziers I settled for a drink instead.

The interior is extremely impressive, loftier than any other cathedral in France with the exception of Amiens and Beauvais. Mansart designed the huge altar. There are eighteenth-century choir stalls and a superb organ, as well as Aubusson tapestries.

The cathedral cloister and the archbishop's kitchen (with a massive central pillar) are a reminder of the powerful medieval baron-bishops of Narbonne. The kitchen's romanesque capitals depict the infant Jesus, Mary, Joseph, Elizabeth embracing Mary – all the gentleness of the Christian story (perhaps a curious setting from which to feed the court of determined prelates who claimed the presidency of the Languedoc estates general by right).

The rue de l'Ancre leads from the cathedral to the archbishops' palace. (There is a real anchor let into the wall of the street.) The archbishops' palace was restored by Viollet-le-Duc, and curiously enough is two palaces in one: an old one, begun in the tenth century and finished at the renaissance, and a 'new' one built in the second half of the fourteenth century.

A plaque in the palace courtyard recalls long-dead troubadours of the Languedoc. Everything is magically irregular. To the left is the art and history museum, reached by a staircase of 1628; to the right the archaeological museum, which incorporates the chapel of Saint-Mary-Magdalen, with an inscription to Pierre de Montbrun who built it in 1273 and with fourteenth-century frescoes depicting St Just and the Annunciation. And opposite the palace is a late nineteenth-century shopping precinct, courteously dedicated *Aux Dames de France*.

Just north of the cathedral, at No. 16 rue Rouget-de-l'Isle, is an unusual survival: the Horreum Romain, a cool (well, cold) Roman underground grain store. Narbonne was founded around 600 BC, and this subterranean museum (for that is what it has become) seems to let one step back almost that far in time.

Beyond the Roman granary is the (happily well signposted) old quarter of the city. This area of narrow winding streets boasts modern shops selling sophisticated woollens, an old shoemaker's, a *salon de thé*, houses holding each other up, *créperies*, hamburger emporia and many elegant balconies. Through it flows the River Aude, fronted by bars and restaurants and with four rows of plane trees creating a shady promenade.

The memory of the over-mighty archbishops of Narbonne usually persuades me to drive southwest for a visit to the restored abbey of Fontfroide, founded in the eleventh century and retaining an entrancing cloister. Or you could go south to Sigean on the motorway, where there is an African safari park, sheltering prides of lions, zebras, rhinos, giraffes, one elephant, and countless antelopes.

Another good excursion from Béziers is to take the same motorway northeast, leaving it after 32 kilometres for Pézenas.

Pézenas has a tourist department with the excellent

Reliefs by David d'Angers decorating the graceful mid nineteenth-century theatre at Béziers.

Above **The warm stones of Capendu, west of Narbonne.**

Right **A superb apotheosis of the Virgin Mary in the cloister of Narbonne cathedral.**

Left The Canal de la Robine at Narbonne.

Above The cloister of Fontfroide, rebuilt in the seventeenth century as the monks' wealth increased.

The elegant house of a seventeenth-century administrator of the Languedoc at Pézenas.

Graceful ironwork and a glum face in the place Gambetta, Pézenas.

policy of discreetly labelling every building, making it a hundred times easier for visitors to enjoy what there is to be seen without having to constantly refer to a guidebook. The wide cours Jean-Jaurès which bisects the town, leading northwest from the place de la République, is refreshingly planted with acacias rather than the usual plane trees. Turn right at the end into the exquisite old town, dating from the fifteenth to the eighteenth centuries, with a Jewish ghetto thrown in. These days every imaginable trinket seems to be on sale. Pézenas even boasts a glass-blower. The shops sell a local delicacy, sweets called *Berlingots de Pézenas*, flavoured in aniseed, chocolate, coffee, strawberry and caramel. Look out for renaissance carvings on the corners of the streets, wrought-iron balconies, cool courtyards and fabulous doorways. A rebellion against Richelieu was fomented in the place Gambetta here in 1632, the rebellion that cost the Duke of Montmorency

his life (see p. 72) and Pézenas its château.

Opposite the sixteenth-century former town hall (*maison des consuls*) in the *place* is the house of a seventeenth-century barber named Gély, remembered today for his merry friendship with the playwright Molière. Armand de Bourbon, Prince de Conti and governor of the Languedoc, was a discriminating patron of the arts and fostered Molière's career. As a result, Molière's company paid frequent visits to Pézenas between the years 1650 and 1657. Molière would stay with Gély, sitting on the sofa, listening to visitors relating eloquent anecdotes, telling tales of his own. Here he wrote *Les précieuses ridicules*. Then, alas,

Shady streets in Pézenas, welcome escape from the summer sun.

the prince's priggish wife turned Conti against the theatre. Molière came here no more.

Pézenas has more than made up for this slight on French drama and each year mounts a Mirondela (*langue d'oc* for parade) of the arts. For two months every summer, members of the celebrated Comédie Française come to direct and star in French classical drama. I went to see *L'École des Femmes*, that profoundly witty insight into the relations between the sexes which Molière wrote in 1662, the year he took a wife twenty years his junior.

The church of Saint-Jean at Pézenas is well worth seeing, standing opposite the main entrance of the sixteenth-century house of the Knights of St John of Jerusalem. The mighty rococo organ was built in 1759 by the Toulouse master Jean-François l'Épine, who had married a local girl.

The truth is that both this town and the area round about have an abundance of rich churches in lovely medieval settings. At Montagnac, 6 kilometres east, tall narrow streets with ancient buildings lead to the bizarre open network tower of the thirteenth- and fourteenth-century church, whose delicate arched doorway is carved with little faces peering down at you as you go in. From the outside you can clearly see three levels of building: the lower part rough stone and filled-in arches; then a layer of smooth stones; then gothic decoration. Inside, there is a noble pulpit and gleaming nineteenth-century glass.

In the opposite direction, 10 kilometres northwest, lies Caux. Here the massive arcaded belfry of the church is set alongside huge black ramparts pierced with a lovely single arch. Drive from here to Nizas (with a twelfth-century château) and then north to Paulhan, from where the main road leads further north to Clermont-l'Hérault. Whichever way you look you see vineyard after vineyard.

I stayed a night at the rustic hotel at Paulhan. As at Millas, there are two clocks here, one on the romanesque church, the other on the market hall, one chiming the hours 45 seconds after the other, but this insomniac's nightmare was more than outweighed by the pleasure of eating dinner under the trees in the hotel garden. I drank a fruity white Languedoc wine from the local château la Condamine-Bertrand, which was pleasing enough. The patronne told me that all the children automatically learn Spanish at school here. And her husband, a gastronomic genius with great moustaches, introduced me to a remarkable and yet simple delicacy, *Feuilleté Roquefort*. He took some cheese, mixed it with cream, wrapped it in puff pastry, and heated it in the oven for ten minutes or so. I followed this by eating his succulent quails cooked in a big potato.

Roquefort, by universal agreement the king of cheeses, is the result of mixing milk from the sheep of Lacauze with a baccillus found in the caves at Roquefort-sur-Soulzon, on the north face of Mont Combalou in the Tarn northwest of Toulouse. It is not known who first thought of this unusual combination, but even in Gallo-Roman times the fissures were used to cultivate the unique baccillus (*penicillium Roque-forti*), that created a cheese praised by Caesar and Pliny alike. Charlemagne had Roquefort delivered to Aix-la-Chapelle. Their cheese cannot have been quite like ours, for both the production and quality of Roquefort were boosted by the development of a new breed of Lacauze sheep in the eighteenth century.

Today three companies specialize in the manufacture of this delicacy, together producing annually some 16,000 tonnes of cheese, using 65 million litres of milk from 800,000 sheep.

Clermont-l'Hérault already boasted three churches in 586. Seven hundred years later the citizens decided to combine the three parishes into one and constructed the massive church of Saint-Paul with its three beautifully vaulted aisles. The many troubles of this unhappy region over the centuries have marked the church. Accused of Cathar heresy in 1324, the people tried to prove their orthodoxy by constructing a huge rose window with stained glass depicting a chalice and the host – for the Cathars rejected the orthodox sacraments of the Church. (That glass has gone, and the present glass dates from 1955.) In 1351 the marauding English forced the townspeople to construct a mighty machicolated tower for the defence of their church, and to add machicolations to its west end. They built a way into these machicolations over the rose window, and everything was then united with the city ramparts. Another testimony to hard times at Clermont-l'Hérault is a painting of St Paul falling from his horse, which the people had desperately vowed to commission if they escaped the plague in 1652.

Happier times produced fine church furniture: the gift of a bell to ring the hours in 1585 (the slender clock-tower contrasting gently with the squat defensive one); the pulpit of 1638, offered to the city by the consuls provided that their names were inscribed on it; the eighteenth-century high altar, crucifix and statues. In 1766 a new door was opened at the west end.

A little fish and vegetable market sets itself up each morning to the north of the church, with a bigger one on Wednesdays. I like to buy a picnic here and then set out for the countryside, in particular a drive around the lake of Salagou. You leave the cathedral by way of rue Doyen-René-Gosse, turning right at the bottom of the street and right again at the sign for Salagou.

After 100 metres another signpost points to Salagou. For a more interesting route it is better to continue along the D908 towards Villeneuvette, the 'little new town' founded by Colbert in 1677 to weave cloth for army uniforms. The trade finished only in 1954, and today this entrancing spot – an entirely homogeneous walled town – is a centre for horseback-riding.

Drive west of Villeneuvette, looking out for the D8E where you turn right for the spectacular 'dolomite circuit' of Mourèze – grotesque, contorted limestone rocks, chiselled and sculpted by atmospheric erosion, with the ancient village of Mourèze perched amongst them. The region is well signposted for walks. Nearby are the remains of an impressive Roman town.

On the road to Salasc from here, as it swings right at the corner, there is a proud memorial to 105 members of the Bir Hakeim resistance group, killed by the Nazis in this region between 1944 and 1945. Some of them are listed by their nicknames: 'Papillon', 'Micko'. One has no name at all (recorded simply as *Inconnu tué à la parade*'). Listed among them is the so-called 'English

major', save that his name is inscribed 'Captain Fowler'. The monument has a legend: 'Tell our young ones not to despair of life, for in difficult times we have shown that we can live, fight and die with dignity.'

Continue along the 'dolomite circuit', through tiny Salasc with its twelfth-century church, little renaissance château and a fountain in the square. The countryside changes colour now, with laval mountains rearing up. (The route to take is the D148 to Octon.) To the right is the huge lake of Salagou, created in 1959 when the Hérault authorities decided to dam the river of the same name. This is now a tourist centre, with surfing and sailing, though the lake is also bordered by a dead, lava-built shanty-town. Soon the colour of the landscape changes again, turning from black to red.

At the N9 turn left for Lodève and cross the river into the old city. I once spent a night here since I wanted to enjoy a trumpet and organ concert in the massively buttressed former cathedral (reached up the Grand'Rue that is always alive with stalls and shops). The town hall next to the cathedral has two gaily tiled roofs. Lodève displays many fine balconies, and one in particular intrigues me. In rue 4 Septembre, near the cathedral, is a metal balcony, signed by B. Cusson, depicting the busts of Benvenuto Cellini, Raphael and Michelangelo in roundels.

Lodève is near the high point of Languedoc monasticism, the superb medieval village of Saint-Guilhem-le-Désert. A good route takes you through Saint-Félix-de-Lodez – still partly fortified and retaining its thirteenth-century church – and the renaissance and classical town of Saint-André-de-Sangonis, where you turn left along the D4 to Saint-Jean-de-Fos.

Saint-Jean-de-Fos was first mentioned in written history in 804. Its ramparts and gate date from the thirteenth century, its church from a century earlier. And the devil's bridge across the River Hérault, built from 1036 to 1048, is the oldest medieval bridge in France. Close by is the subterranean cavern of Clamouse, which can be visited.

Saint-Guilhem-le-Désert suddenly appears on the left, amid towering white cliffs. You can park at the top

Above **The lake of Salagou near Clermont-l'Hérault.**

Right **The devil's bridge crosses the River Hérault south of Saint-Guilhem-le-Désert. Built in 1036–48, it was enlarged two centuries later.**

of the village (or *cité*, as it calls itself), and then walk down to the abbey of Gellone. This is named after Charlemagne's ally Guilhem (known as 'the Short-nose', since the tip of his nose was cut off when he was despatching a wild Saracen), who fought valiantly with the sword for the Christian faith. He then decided to fight the spiritual combat instead and founded the abbey here in 804 under the inspiration of the Benedictines at nearby Aniane. Charlemagne gave the abbey a piece of the true cross, which you can still see inside the cool twelfth-century church.

Guilhem (who is known as Guillaume d'Orange in medieval epic poems) died in 812. Soon he was venerated as a saint. Just round the corner of the right-hand pillar where the relic of the true cross is venerated is an eighteenth-century polychrome carving depicting his two heroes: St Benedict of Nursia (480–547, founder of the Benedictines) and St Benedict of Aniane (751–821, reformer of the order and Guilhem's inspiration).

The relics of Guilhem himself were transferred from the crypt to the choir in 1138 and placed in a marble sarcophagus, but most of his bones were flushed away in a flood of 1817. There are only a couple of wings of the abbey cloisters, with the refectory and a fish pool, but even these remnants seem exquisite. (To enjoy what is missing you must go to New York, since parts were sold to the Americans after the abbey was suppressed at the Revolution. Cardinal de Cabrière bought the abbey back from the State in 1910.)

By the twelfth century a village was growing up outside the abbey. Leave the church and cloister (shaded by a huge plane tree planted in 1848 which is now nearly 5.6 metres in circumference) to explore its narrow streets. The many delights include the Chapel of the White Penitents, the former church of Saint-Laurent (now the village hall), the ruined prison, old monastic latrines, and shady medieval houses.

A longish, spectacular ride takes you northwest alongside the Hérault gorge (with many places to swim and canoe) by way of Saint-Bauzille-de-Putois to the remarkable Grotte des Demoiselles, an astonishingly convoluted and cavernous underground cave, with a funicular railway carrying you up inside the mountain. The guided tour lasts about an hour and takes you up and down some 550 steps.

The speleologist Edouard Martel rediscovered this cave in 1931, though it is believed that the eighteenth-century Protestants knew of it and hid here from their Catholic persecutors. Long ago, as prehistoric finds indicate, some of our earliest ancestors found shelter here too.

To my mind there are only two problems about visiting these fascinating caves: first, the French habitually take their dogs along for the tour; secondly, the guides are frequently the most exasperating persons imaginable.

My guide at the Grotte des Demoiselles was no exception. Instead of telling us useful information (such as that the colours of these stalagmites and stalactites, when blue, derive from manganese oxide, when red from iron oxide, when green from the effects of human breath), instead of trying to explain why some stalagmites are translucent and others not, instead of expounding on how we manage to date these powerful encrustations, he poured out fanciful rubbish comparing one cavern to a cathedral, one huge mass of stalagmite to a pulpit, another group to the Virgin and Child, another to a flock of sheep, finally finishing off his maunderings with a pathetic attempt to use some little stalactites as a xylophone.

In my view what he called the tympanum of the pulpit, if it must be compared with anything, looked more like the upper jaw of a crocodile. Yet so all-pervasive has this nonsense become that at Christmas the local parish priest celebrates midnight Mass in this 'cathedral'.

The return to Montpellier should take in two superb churches, Saint-Martin-de-Londres and Saint-Sauveur at Aniane. The first – a perfect romanesque church in a village of arcades and little tunnels – is reached by taking the D986 south from the Grotte des Demoiselles.

The romanesque church doorway and the place de l'Eglise at Saint-Martin-de-Londres.

Above **The dilapidated wash-house at Aniane.**

Left **Arcades and tunnels conjure up a medieval past at Saint-Martin-de-Londres.**

Then leave Saint-Martin-de-Londres to the south, the Montagne de la Celette rising in front, and take the D32 right through the impressively fortified village of Viols-le-Fort. This region is a paradise for pre-historians, littered with dolmens and tumuli and prehistoric caves. The road passes by the strong walls of Puéchabon, which has expanded a little since the fourteenth century but preserves a complex, hostile château with mighty ramparts at its heart.

At the T-junction turn left to Aniane. Charlemagne's cup-bearer, Benedict, son of Aigulf of Maguelone, retired to this spot in the early ninth century to live in solitude by a brook, meditating on the holy life and eventually reforming the whole Benedictine order.

The surprise is that the hermitage of the saint who inspired Saint-Guilhem-le-Désert has developed not into a peaceful monastic village but into a bustling town with a splendid late seventeenth-, early eighteenth-century church. Don't miss the terrific classical façade of Saint-Sauveur (with the lower storey held up by four Doric columns and that above by four Corinthian ones). For me the high points of the interior are its eighteenth-century 'gothic' roof bosses and the cherubs of the arcades. As for the seventeenth-century monastic buildings, after the Revolution they became public property and were used first as a factory and then as a detention centre. Today they house a reform school.

From Aniane drive 5 kilometres south to Gignac, another bustling seventeenth- and eighteenth-century town with fine contemporary churches. The N109 now takes you directly back into Montpellier, running alongside Pitot's lovely aqueduct.

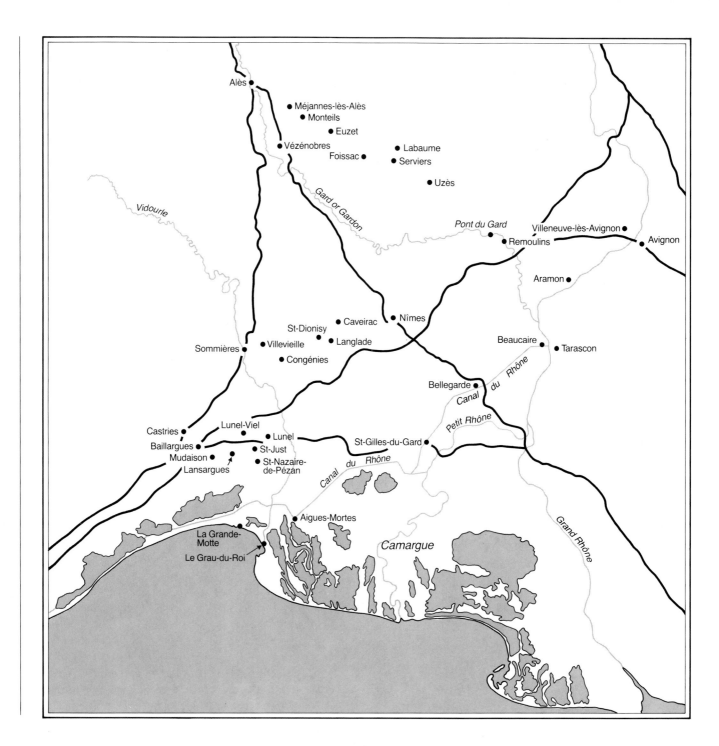

5
A Somnolent Savage Land

*Nîmes – Sommières – Aigues-Mortes – the
Camargue – Beaucaire – Villeneuve-lès-Avignon –
the Pont du Gard – Uzès*

'I was born on the 13 May 1840 in a city of the Languedoc, Nîmes, where are to be found – as in all the cities of the Midi – a great deal of sunshine, quite a lot of dust, a Carmelite convent, and two or three Roman remains.' So wrote Alphonse Daudet in his autobiographical novel *Le Petit Chose (Little What's His Name).*

Times do change, not much in the Midi, but nevertheless a little. I arrived at Nîmes one evening in August extremely pleased with myself at having booked a very reasonably priced room at Le Lisita, a hotel exactly adjacent to the great Roman amphitheatre itself, only to find that I was assailed all evening by blaring music. This came from a no-doubt excellent show (named *Holiday on Ice*) that was being staged within that venerable arena, where the citizens of Augustus Caesar had watched games and gladiators. It was little comfort to me that at least those taking part were not tormenting a fine bull.

I think I went to sleep happily. At least I had forgotten *Holiday on Ice* by the time I had sampled some of the local specialities at dinner.

Nîmes has grown contented and perhaps sleepy on the rich food of the Midi. The soup I ate that evening was *le pistou*, rich with the garlic, pasta, fresh basil, olive oil and vegetables that make men's faces swarthy here. This I followed with a cod *soufflé*, if that is the right word for *brandade de morue*, in which pounded

cod is mixed with olive oil, hot milk and a pinch of garlic, and served with fried croûtons and a dash of lemon juice and nutmeg. You can eat *brandade* elsewhere in the Languedoc (though the *langue d'oc* nickname for the people of Nîmes is *manjo merlusso*, 'cod-eaters'). What makes a *brandade* recipe special to this city is the garlic.

Even though I was feasting on fish, I drank almost a bottle of the local red wine (which is called Costières-du-Gard and so far as I know has not been awarded any sort of *appellation contrôlée*). It helped me to ignore *Holiday on Ice*, and a glass of the *pastis* much loved in Nîmes washed the noise away altogether. (I suppose I ought to have drunk the *pastis* as an apéritif, but I didn't.) Next morning, in consequence, I awoke in an excellent frame of mind.

Even if you don't have the benefit of a superb meal inside you, exploring Nîmes reveals delights almost at every turn, the product of centuries of civilized living. Nîmes was originally inhabited by a Celtic tribe who worshipped the deity of a spring here. The deity came to be called Nemausus, hence Nîmes.

But the Romans soon took over, veterans of Octavian's army that had defeated Cleopatra's lovesick Antony. Nîmes has an Egyptian crocodile chained to a palm tree in its coat of arms, to remind itself of that victory. Quintessentially Nîmes is an Augustan city,

153

with the finest preserved Roman remains (some, like the arena and the Maison Carrée, still in use).

Like the Celts, the Romans used the spring as a water supply and (as an inscription of 25 BC reveals) for its healing properties. But they also embellished it beautifully. In the second, or perhaps the third century AD they built a curious but elegant double open doorway facing the spring. Close by two temples were constructed, one to Nemausus and the other – since Roman emperors expected to be deified after death (if not before) – to Augustus. The spring itself is housed in a fine *nymphaeum* (fountain-house), adorned with statues. An altar to the god was placed inside the open doorways. The Romans also built the so-called Temple of Diana. Here the devout (or superstitious) would sleep, having prayed that the god of the spring would miraculously visit them overnight to cure any ailment from which they might be suffering.

This Temple of Diana still exists, though partly ruined. In contrast the arena or amphitheatre is in almost perfect condition, paradoxically, it seems, preserved by misuse.

The arena at Nîmes was constructed in the first century AD. A perfect ellipse, it is 133 metres long and 101 metres wide. Each level of steps, 24 in all, seated 1000 spectators. The Romans calculated that the average person was wide enough to sit on no more than 40 centimetres, and each spectator was allotted exactly that. The Romans were also acutely conscious of social differences, so the various orders were carefully segregated in separate parts of the arena. The inscriptions indicating where the great ones sat have been removed to the museum of archaeology.

By the time of the Visigoths the original purpose of the arena was virtually forgotten. But whereas other Roman arenas were dismantled (at least in part) by people looking for convenient building materials, the arena at Nîmes became a military bastion which was lived in by officers of the army. There was even an

A corridor of the amphitheatre at Nîmes displays the skills of the Roman architects.

official military company, the chevaliers des Arènes. Churches were built inside the great walls.

Finally the poor colonized it, 2000 of them, building houses inside its walls, filling the amphitheatre with their detritus, and inadvertently protecting the ancient stones until most of the site was excavated in 1809. The great stones, quarried at Barutel 7 kilometres outside Nîmes, reappeared in their pristine glory.

Walking around the outside is a breathtaking experience. The walls are two storeys high, the sixty vigorous arcades of the lower storey supported on square pilasters, those of the upper storey on Doric columns. Of the four entrances at the four points of the compass, so to speak, the principal gate in Roman times was on the north, while today we use the west. Is this the reason why this hard stone, so difficult to cut, has a few carvings on the north side by the original entrance – the she-wolf suckling Romulus and Remus, gladiators fighting, a couple of bulls?

The brilliance of the design, with interior galleries and special alleys reserved for the amphitheatre staff, is awe-inspiring. The wings – like those in modern theatres – must have been used to work some sort of scenery, since a couple of lead counterweights have been found here. Sockets at the top of the whole edifice supported a huge awning sheltering spectators from the sun that shines here for ten months out of twelve. The staff responsible for erecting this awning could reach it by a hidden flight of steps without disturbing the audience. The audience could move around with greater ease than in most twentieth-century theatres.

And to me it is delightful that we almost certainly know the name of the man who built the arena. On one of the walls of the gallery are inscribed the words:

T CRISPIVS REBVRRVS FECIT
(Titus Crispius Reburrus made it)

For those who like low, unequal bloodthirsty sports I ought to add that the first modern bullfights took place here in 1863. The Nîmois and Nîmoïses – both men and women – love them.

Today the sadism involved is masked by beautifully conceived rituals. The first great Corrida of the year at

Nîmes takes place at Pentecost, when it is given a religious patina. Two more are presented in August and at the end of September. As a preliminary to the real action, red capes (or *véroniques*) are deployed to enrage the bulls. Next picadors mounted on blindfolded padded old nags stick their spikes into the doomed animals. Then the *banderillos* ride in and plant hooked spears into the beasts' necks. The climax of this graceful savagery comes with the *tercio de muerte*, when an exquisitely dressed matador, his épée concealed in his cape, performs a classically dangerous dance of death with the weakened bull, before killing it – usually after several thrusts. I have heard matadors viciously hissed and vociferously decried for inadvertently killing a bull with the first thrust. Naturally, I was too shy to be the sole spectator applauding the early despatch of the tormented and exhausted beast when I once watched the show here.

In these bullfights Spain has overlaid Rome at Nîmes. At times the Nîmois seem to exude an air of softness, almost a suggestion of somnolence, and I often ask myself whether this does not conceal an inner violence – perhaps a legacy of a violent past. Certainly there is a virtuous softness about the whole of the Midi, and this is manifested most strongly in Nîmes.

This characteristic quality seems to have been recognized by Alphonse Daudet, whose city this was. Daudet's childhood and youth were marred by poverty, and he escaped to make his way in Paris at the age of seventeen. He was keenly aware of the difference between north and south, and could write movingly about their contrasting attitudes to the profound elements of life, such as love:

'If we look at that most violent of human passions, love, we see that the southerner makes of love the main occupation of his life, but does not allow himself to be thrown out of kilter by it. He likes the gossip in it, the light frills and the changing faces. He detests the servitude it brings. For him it becomes a pretext for serenades and dissertations, for indulging in teasing and caresses. Only with difficulty can he comprehend the connection between love and death which exists at the bottom of every northern soul and throws a mist of melancholy over its brief delights.'

True perhaps; but none the less southerners were thrown totally out of kilter several times by the very religion which declared that God is love. When the Arian heresy reached Nîmes, it provoked Christian to turn viciously on fellow-Christian. The barbarian invaders savaged the city. The godly Charles Martel even tried to set fire to the amphitheatre. The Cathars infested the city and were bloodily suppressed.

Seemingly needing to take reprisals on some innocent bystanders, the Nîmois threw the Jews out of the city in 1349, although they had been there for six centuries. Nîmes turned Protestant at the Reformation, and in 1567 the Protestants celebrated St Michael's Day by massacring most of the Catholics. For some reason I cannot understand, the city remained reasonably calm during the Revolution, but made up for it in 1815 when murderous reprisals were incited by the returning nobility.

Yet Nîmes has also nurtured brave men and women who fought for good causes. Opposite the amphitheatre stand the modern law courts. A plaque on one corner commemorates two twenty-year-old *maquisards*, Jean Robert and Vincent Faita, killed by the Nazis on 22 April 1945.

You can walk to the celebrated Maison Carrée from this sad memorial by a picturesque route through old Nîmes. Take the rue de l'Aspic, where a curious four-legged man is set on the corner of the street, a bizarre modern construction made out of several different antique remains. From this street a right turn along the rue de l'Hôtel de Ville will bring you to the town hall, which sports a clock with a jolly Chinaman ringing the hours and quarters. The clock was made by Jacquemart in 1880 and seems perfectly at ease with the eighteenth-century façade of the building on which it sits. This square is in fact a pleasing mixture of all sorts of styles: note the dogs, the wild boar and the couple of hinds sculpted on one of the houses.

An old covered passageway (the rue de la Trésorie, with the medieval flank of the town hall running down it) leads to the rue Dorée, a shady street with some marvellous classical doorways opening into quiet courtyards. If the doors of No. 16 (the former Hôtel de l'Académie) are open, don't fail to go inside to admire the balconies and balustraded staircase.

A short way down a street to the left is the former Jesuit chapel, an architectural masterpiece designed by Père de Mourges in the 1670s with superbly worked iron balconies. It seems perfectly suited for its present function of housing a museum of religious art.

The chapel cloister has been imaginatively turned into a museum of lapidary art. This seems to me a lovely setting for ancient sarcophagi, mosaics, busts, funeral stones and torsos. Among them all I find the touching mosaic of an unfortunate man being run over by a chariot very moving.

Other rooms of the former monastery exhibit ethnology and prehistory: the skeleton of an extinct species of bear; bracelets; ancient smashed pots carefully glued together; neolithic axes; Bronze Age weapons; needles; prehistoric menhirs carved with quaint, sad faces. One of the most praiseworthy elements of these rooms is that their curators do not try to show you too much. I felt not the slightest intellectual indigestion here.

To reach Nîmes cathedral from here, go down the Grand'Rue, turning left along the rue du Chapitre. The former episcopal palace (1685) is now a museum of old Nîmes. I have picnicked in its garden but never ventured inside.

Pope Urban II consecrated the romanesque cathedral of Our Lady and Saint Castor in 1096. Much ravaged over the centuries, especially during the Wars of Religion, it was restored in a very cold romanesque style in the late nineteenth century. The huge square tower with its gothic belfry dates from the fifteenth century. There is one feature of this building which particularly entrances me. High up on the left of the façade in the place aux Herbes are sculptures of Adam and Eve, Cain and Abel and the death of Abel – all romanesque originals. Had I not read that the sculptures on the right are an eighteenth-century attempt to imitate the romanesque, would I have spotted the difference?

Opposite the cathedral façade is the rue de la Madeleine, with a twelfth-century romanesque house at No. 1. If you follow this street you reach the church of Saint-Eugénie on the left, which strangely I have always found shut on Sundays. Its nineteenth-century façade fronts a romanesque nave.

Turn right to reach the place de l'Horloge, with its eighteenth-century clock-tower. This square is the birthplace of a man who has been responsible for millions of premature deaths and whose malign influence lives on today. Jean Nicot, French ambassador to Portugal, introduced tobacco to France and the word nicotine to the Western world.

From here a short walk leads by way of the rue de la Madeleine to the boulevard Victor-Hugo, in which stands the church of Saint-Paul. At Mass here one Sunday I was relieved to find that the lines of the neo-romanesque building designed by Charles Questel in the mid nineteenth century, together with the paintings by Hippolyte Flandrin, were interesting enough to divert me during an unusually tedious sermon.

Walk right along the boulevard Victor-Hugo to reach the superlative Maison Carrée, built in AD 5. (The translation 'square house' will not do, for the Maison Carrée was named when 'carrée' also meant 'oblong', and the house is not quite square.) It was dedicated to the sons of Agrippa, himself the son-in-law of the Emperor Augustus. We know this because in 1785 a diligent Nîmes archaeologist traced the holes left by some long disappeared bronze letters and deciphered the following inscription:

C CAESARI AVGVSTI F COS L CAESAR F COS
DESIGNATO
PRINCIPIBVS IVVENTVTIS

(To Caius Caesar, son of Augustus, consul, to Lucius Caesar, son of Augustus, nominated consul: to the princes of youth)

The word used is 'son', but it actually means 'grandson'.

The Maison Carrée became national property at the French Revolution and its design inspired the monumental church of the Madeleine, Paris, built to the glory of Napoleon. In 1816 the authorities wisely

decided to transform this marvellously preserved Roman temple into a museum and art gallery, and such it remains to this day.

You read a lot about the perfect proportions of Roman buildings; the Maison Carrée proves it all true. The late eighteenth-century observer Arthur Young, who confessed that he had met with 'piles of laboured foppery and heaviness' in French architecture, thought it beyond all comparison the most light, elegant, and pleasing building he had ever seen. He added:

'There is a magic harmony in the proportions that charms the eye. One can fix no particular part of pre-eminent beauty; it is one perfect whole of symmetry and grace.'

It is worth pausing to work out the mathematics of this chaste and elegant beauty (25.5 metres long, 13.5 metres wide, 17 metres high). Every dimension of the Maison Carrée is related to another in a ratio of two to one, or three to one: the length is twice as long as the width; the height consists of a podium exactly a third the height of the Corinthian columns and a superstructure exactly as high as the podium.

When built, the Maison Carrée was opposite the Roman forum, now the site of the rue Auguste. This leads to a statue of Antoninus Pius, who was born in this city and became emperor in AD 138.

To the left is the flower-bordered canal, which leads to the elegantly concealed reason for the whole existence of Nîmes, the spring of the god Nemausus. It is concealed because the consuls of the city authorized the construction of a canal in 1738 in order to provide a more reliable and abundant source of water, and this somewhat diminishes the significance of the old fountain. It is elegant because they commissioned the military engineer Jacques-Philippe Mareschal to surround the fountain with gardens. The result is a superb promenade, with a statue of the nymph of the spring by Dominique Roché presiding over it all.

The perfectly proportioned Maison Carrée built at Nîmes in AD 5.

While the workmen were constructing this garden, they discovered the Roman ruin which we now call the Temple of Diana. (Nobody knows what its original name was.) Its history since Roman times had been bizarre. It was transformed in 994 into a nuns' convent and then half demolished during the Wars of Religion. Half a century later some of its remaining stones were cannibalized to build the city walls.

The consuls of 1750 were delighted at its discovery, and hoped at first to restore it. They failed, I'm happy to say, for this is a most romantic ruin; and if anyone still believes that Roman architecture was straightforward and unsubtle, this is the antidote – delicate pediments of alternating patterns, finely chiselled door surrounds, an ornamental central hall flanked by gracefully proportioned corridors.

A monumental flight of steps leads from the garden to the great tower (or *tour magne*), the finest of the nineteen towers built on the rampart which the Romans threw round the city. The Roman walls at Nîmes were the longest in all Gaul – 7 kilometres in all, 3 metres thick at the base. Part of the circuit can still be seen on the road from Nîmes to Alès, but this tower and the gate of Augustus are its noblest remnants.

Nearly 34 metres high, shaped like a polygon at the base, it once was even more impressive. One of the numerous failed prophecies of the astrologer Nostradamus helped to destroy part of it. Nostradamus had proclaimed that a gardener would excavate a treasure in Nîmes. In 1601 a local gardener, conceiving that the prophecy applied exclusively to him, started pulling down the tower in order to dig under it. Fortunately he was stopped before the *tour magne* was totally demolished.

To find the gate of Augustus you must walk back along the quayside of the canal de la Fontaine and down the rue Nationale. The gate stands at the point where the Via Domitiana reached Nîmes (the rue Nationale now follows the line of the Roman road exactly). Two openings on either side are wide enough for pedestrians; two in the middle were for horse-drawn vehicles.

Once again scholars have worked out exactly when

Left Part of the eighteenth-century fountain in the gardens of Nîmes.

Above The hostile towers and walls defending Aigues-Mortes conjure up the brooding spirit of the thirteenth century.

161

this gate was placed here by transcribing the holes left by the bronze letters which once adorned it. These read:

IMP CAESAR DIVI F AVGVSTVS COS XI TRIB
POTEST VIII
PORTAS MVRAS COL DAT
(Caesar Augustus, emperor, son of the divine [i.e Julius Caesar], consul for the eleventh time, granted the power of tribune for the eighth time, gives these gates to the town)

Since Augustus was granted the power of tribune for the eighth time in 16 BC, that exactly dates the great gate.

For a tour of the surrounding area leave Nîmes by the D40 and drive west to picturesque Sommières, which Lawrence Durrell described as the most beautiful town in the Languedoc.

The route leads through some entrancing, yet virtually unknown villages. Caveirac was mentioned in written history as early as 893. Its twelfth-century church has a pretty doorway, its château dates from the seventeenth century. Langlade is even older, with a rectangular Roman site to prove it. Saint-Dionisy sports another twelfth-century church, redone in the seventeenth. Congénies is also blessed with a twelfth-century church. Just outside Sommières you pass the Château de Villevieille, its medieval towers and renaissance façade peering down at the River Vidourle from a rocky precipice.

The town of Sommières grew up where a Roman bridge (many times restored) crosses the Vidourle. The main street, running from this bridge, leads from a lower market to an upper market. Sommières is a town of arcades and old gateways, of plane trees and vaulted little streets. No longer menacing, the ruined medieval château still looks down on the town and it is worth climbing up to it to get the view over the rooftops. Here, it is said, the Revolutionaries locked up loose women who were rendering the citizens unfit to serve their fatherland.

Fifteen kilometres southwest of Sommières is Castries, a name which rightly suggests that the settlement started life as a Roman camp (*castrum*) on the Via Domitiana. For those who have time to spare, a round tour of seven towns beyond Castries would keep architectural afficionados profitably and enjoyably occupied for a week.

From Castries take the D26 southeast to Baillargues, an enchanting place with an eighteenth-century château and a romanesque church whose fortifications contrast quaintly with the fourteenth-century decorated doorway. The high altar was brought here from the Franciscan convent at Montpellier in 1793. Further southwest at Mudaison is another twelfth-century church.

The tiny village of Lansargues, east along the D189, has been occupied for centuries, as the Roman villas and Bronze Age site here testify. Here too are the Château Grasset-Morel and two pretty churches, the older one facing not east-west but north-south, the younger one dating from the eighteenth century.

Continue 4 kilometres east to Saint-Nazaire-de-Pézan, which again boasts Roman villas and a château. The church has a couple of pre-romanesque capitals. Just north is Saint-Just, where the architect who built the modern church has incorporated a romanesque west façade.

Drive from Saint-Just northwest along the D110 to Lunel-Viel, with its prehistoric caves, its Visigothic tombs, and its gothic church. From here the N113 runs due east to Lunel, which legend says the Jews founded and which certainly boasts a Jewish academy with roots dating back to the twelfth century. Alas, the town expelled its own Jews in 1298. Lunel has no ramparts since Louis XIII demolished them in 1632 and the stones were used to restore Aigues-Mortes. But nobody has destroyed the medieval houses and a seventeenth-century gothic church.

There is more to see in Castries. Next to the town hall is a ruined old church which fell down in 1870. The citizens have not yet got round to rebuilding it. The classical château here is well worth visiting for its furnished rooms and tapestries, but especially for its superb classical gardens, set out by Le Nôtre on the model of Versailles.

The arcades of the upper market place, Sommières.

The château was given its classical unity by an almost total reconstruction between 1656 and 1676, after the Duke de Rohan had set fire to the old buildings in 1622. An added marvel of Le Nôtre's garden is that Pierre-Paul Riquet built an aqueduct 6882 metres long to water it.

From here it is not far to the Mediterranean, and one of the most prized and monstrous seaside resorts in the world: La Grande-Motte. This was entirely created by the architect Baludier at the behest in 1956 of the inter-ministerial commission to improve tourism on the Languedoc coast. No less a man than General de Gaulle declared La Grande-Motte officially open twelve years later.

Certainly La Grand-Motte has improved tourism: in the summer months this part of the coast is insufferably packed with the cars, caravans and bodies of thousands of holidaymakers. As for the architecture of La Grande-Motte, it consists of pyramidal beehives (or hutches) designed to pack in as many human beings as possible with the greatest possible discomfort. Those who approve describe the design as avant-garde and audacious. When I expressed my disapproval to a patriotic French friend, she was horrified.

If I am in this area I choose to swim further east, at the former fishing village of Le Grau-du-Roi. As everywhere along this coast, it is packed with visitors in summer (it has been the seaside resort for the people of Nîmes since the railway age), but it still retains some of its old charms – with fishing boats and a lighthouse and fine stretches of safe sand. Here I even once indulged in that exhilarating form of self-torture known as windsurfing for an hour or two.

Six kilometres inland along the Rhône-Sète Canal lies the dusty, ancient, altogether remarkable city of Aigues-Mortes, with massive walls round all four sides, one of them running along the canal and all crowned with towers and pierced by great gateways. To me the south wall is the most evocative. Approaching the city from this direction it is easy to imagine it without tourists and to conjure up the brooding spirit of the thirteenth century. The great walls rise from flat marshes scattered with low salt basins (the oldest economic activity of the area) and seemingly dead lagoons (*aquae mortuae* or *eaux mortes*), from which Aigues-Mortes takes its name.

The town received its charter from King Louis in 1246. This was an extremely liberal document, so as to attract vigorous, independent-minded citizens to Aigues-Mortes. Louis also built the tower of Constance here so as to have a proper embarkation point for the Seventh Crusade. He set sail for Egypt with a great fleet amidst elaborate ceremonial on 28 August 1248. But

163

the glamorous crusade came to nothing and the remnants returned. Twenty years later the old king was back at Aigues-Mortes. Instead of presiding over jousts and tournaments, King Louis this time brooded anxiously in his tent. Something like half the number of crusaders as had set sail in 1248 embarked in 1270. On 25 August Louis IX died at Tunis, his camp ravaged by the plague.

In 1272 Aigues-Mortes was laid out as a classic bastide by King Philippe the Bold. A Genoese engineer named Bocanegra built the ramparts, which you can walk around today, their narrow slits still like mean eyes threatening hostile strangers. Fittingly enough, only residents are allowed to drive into the city.

In the early years 10,000 people lived here, but there are only 4500 now, for the waterway between Aigues-Mortes and the sea began to silt up disastrously in the fourteenth century.

Religious fanatics found a new use for the now defunct seaport three centuries later. Catholics imprisoned Huguenot women in the tower of Constance after the Protestants had revolted against the revocation of the Edict of Nantes. One of these unfortunates was kept here for thirty-seven years.

Aigues-Mortes undoubtedly merits a visit on foot. In the central square in 1849 the sculptor Pradier erected a statue of the pious Christian soldier and king who founded it. Nearby, the seventeenth-century Capuchin convent became a café and then a fish shop, but is now an exhibition centre. The parish church has been restored. Rue Gambetta boasts a couple of ancient houses and a hospital founded in 1347. And each August a festival of knights on horseback, carrying lances, evokes the medieval past.

As Henry James put it, Aigues-Mortes can hardly be said to be alive, 'but if it is dead, it is very neatly embalmed'.

Aigues-Mortes may well lie amidst dead lagoons, but it also stands on the borders of one of the most vibrant stretches of wild country in the whole of France: the Camargue. The way to Saint-Gilles-du-Gard from Aigues-Mortes passes through one of the four regions into which the Camargue is divided, the one known as the Petite Camargue.

The sand-dunes, lagoons and swamps of this area are all part of the rich delta of the River Rhône. The Languedoc poet Frédéric Mistral described it as without trees, shades or souls. Over the centuries its boundaries change, as the sea brings its debris, as silt and sand add to a promontory here, as streams bite into a landscape there.

For four months in the Camargue it never rains and the sun beats down mercilessly. Often, too, it is lashed by violent winds – the *mistral*, the *trammontana*, the *cissero*, the *largade*. Only the *largade* is welcomed, for it is a prelude to summer.

This seemingly inhospitable land is an oasis for birds, Romanies and animals. Four hundred different species of birds live here. Thousands more pause to rest on their annual migrations. Herons, hoopoes, green woodpeckers and jays abound, while flocks of flamingoes can turn the sky pink. Some of the flamingoes winter here, but the rest depart for Spain and north Africa as autumn arrives.

The Romanies came here nearly five hundred years ago, exiles from present-day India and Pakistan, but the origins of the Camargue bull are much more obscure. Legend has it that these animals were introduced by Attila the Hun. *Lou biòu*, as he is known in the *langue d'oc*, is a squat powerful beast. The breed was dying out in 1869 when a breeder had the insight to cross it with Spanish Navarre cattle. The new strains gave a fresh strength to the bulls of the Camargue. Today some fifty breeders own Camargue bulls, which they brand and then let roam free.

Unable to resist the Spanish habit of fighting bulls, the people of the Camargue have combined the traditional activity with the humane notion of never killing their noble animals. Their sport – no less exciting than traditional bullfighting – involves snatching a red ribbon from between the animal's horns.

The Rhône-Sète canal north of Aigues-Mortes.

Left **The setting sun above the lagoons and marshes of the Camargue.**

Above **The Camargue is dotted with isolated dwellings such as this.**

And this is the region of the splendid white horses of the Camargue – a unique animal, possibly descended from an early Stone Age species, more likely brought from Arabia by the Moors. Recognize them by their long tails, reaching to the ground; by their bellies, by their speed. With luck you will see a mare, newly emerged from the hiding-place she has chosen to give birth to a foal that is invariably coal black for the first five years of its life. In his poem *Horses of the Camargue* Roy Campbell recounts the legend that an exiled Camargue horse can smell the sea-spray in his native land afar off, when the *mistral* blows. Then:

'. . . in fury, foaming at the rein,
He hurls his rider; and with lifted tail,
With coal-red eyes and cataracting mane,
Heading his course for home,
Though sixty foreign leagues before him sweep,
Will never rest until he breathes the foam,
And hears the native thunder of the deep.'

The best way to explore the Camargue is to do so on horseback. Or stay for a month with binoculars to watch the birds. But for those who are short of time you can get the flavour of the area by driving east from Aigues-Mortes along the D58, turning north and then east again along the D179 which winds to Saint-Gilles-du-Gard.

Windmills still work here. Black cattle graze, the bulls looking up malevolently. I talked to a Camargue farmer who was also a *razeteur*, or bullfighter, during the sporting season. He told me of a friend who made a bull into a pet. Each day he would call the beast, which ran up for a special feed. Each day he would stroke its black nose. One day he stroked it and the beast gored him.

The hedges of the Camargue are centuries old. Streams run beside them, overhung by willows from which the natives weave baskets. Across the meadows of sunflowers the willows are bent by the wind, a mass of silver as their leaves are ruffled by the breeze.

The road into Saint-Gilles-du-Gard crosses the Canal du Rhône, with boats moored against its banks. Drive up to the square of the abbey church and park there. The façade is superb: three romanesque arches, the middle one the largest, separated by a frieze and triple pillars, with a doddery old bell-tower on the right. The three doors, each set under an arch, have splendid metal hinges, curved out so they form part of the decoration.

I wish none the less that these were the original doors of the church, which were given by the pope to St Giles himself on a visit to Rome. To the pope's surprise Giles threw the doors into the River Tiber. The doors then sailed downstream, crossed the Mediterranean, and finally sailed up the River Rhône to land near Giles's little cave.

It was outside the present doors, on 5 January 1208, that the servant of Count Raymond VI of Toulouse murdered the papal legate Peter of Castelnau and so triggered off the Albigensian crusade. Here a year and a half later Raymond himself was flogged in penance for the crime.

In the central arch Christ is portrayed in glory, sitting amidst the four evangelists (or rather, their traditional symbols: a bull, an eagle, a lion and a creature with the face of a human being). This central carving is not in fact original: the Protestants destroyed the first one in the sixteenth century, and the present scene is a seventeenth-century restoration. The lintel below – which runs across the two doors on either side – is original. Although slightly mutilated, it is still beautiful: Judas receives thirty pieces of silver for betraying his Lord; Martha and Mary learn from their friend and Saviour; their brother Lazarus is raised from the dead; Jesus tells a protesting St Peter that Peter will deny him three times. The carving I like best shows Jesus washing the disciples' feet . . . . So the frieze continues, representing all the events of Holy Week, ending with Jesus carrying his cross on the way to be crucified.

Judas betrays Jesus with a kiss, part of the romanesque frieze on the church at Saint-Gilles-du-Gard.

169

Notice that a little foal trots along behind the ass on which he rides into Jerusalem. This is not romanesque sentimentality, a sweet little addition by a soppy sculptor. The artist, like St Matthew in his Gospel, was taking absolutely literally the prophecy of Zechariah:

'Tell the daughter of Zion,
behold, your king is coming to you
humble, and mounted on an ass,
and on a colt, the foal of an ass.'

If the Bible implies that Jesus rode not only on an ass but also on its foal, then a medieval sculptor somehow must deal with that fact – however bizarre it might seem. In my view the sculptor of the frieze of Saint-Gilles-du-Gard has coped exceptionally well, transforming a biblical oddity into a charming natural scene.

St Giles founded a monastery here in the eighth century. The land had been given him by King Wamba of the Visigoths, who had wounded the saint's pet doe while hunting, pursued the little creature to Giles's cell and was overcome with remorse.

Pope Urban II consecrated the altar of a new abbey church in 1096. In the next century merchants, pilgrims, money-changers (more than a hundred of them), hosteliers, pardoners, knights and great ladies came to Saint-Gilles, drawn by the sanctity of its founder. St Louis visited this holy place in 1254. Thereafter the story is one of decline – the abbey suffered much mutilation in the Wars of Religion, in 1622 and after the Revolution. But much – miraculously – remains, especially this west end and the crypt built so that pilgrims could venerate the tomb of St Giles.

The west end puzzles as well as entrances me. Why are the pillars all designed differently – some fluted, some square, some round, one surmounted by an eagle, the other by a human face? What is the significance of the multitude of animals that crawls above the pillars, with an occasional human being peeping out between them?

Inside the church are two gems – a romanesque spiral staircase, and the crypt. The crypt is a church in itself, evidence of how many pilgrims once crowded here to venerate the bones of St Giles.

For many years the saint's body and tomb were lost, but the tomb was found in 1865 and you can see it there today, inscribed:

INH TOML QI CB AEGD

This is shorthand, so to speak, for 'In hoc tumulo quiescit corpus beati Aegidii' ('In this tomb lies the body of the blessed Giles'). In the vault above, Christ blesses pilgrims and today's more secular visitors from the central boss.

If the great tithe barn nearby is anything to go by, the abbey church of Saint-Gilles-du-Gard must have become rich, not simply from pilgrims but also from tithes exacted from the surrounding farmers.

Opposite the church a sign points the way to the romanesque house of Saint-Gilles-du-Gard. A long tradition says that this tall twelfth-century building once belonged to the troubadour Gui Foulques who became Pope Clement VI in 1265. There are other twelfth-century houses elsewhere in this village and in France, but what makes this one rare is its decoration – every window differently carved, simple but satisfying.

Join the D38 and drive northeast to Beaucaire, passing through Bellegarde with its watermills and its sad thirteenth-century château, once belonging to the knights of St John of Jerusalem.

The legendary town of Beaucaire lies on the right bank of the Rhône on the Via Domitiana, directly opposite Tarascon. There was a Bronze Age site on this spot and then the settlement flourished greatly under the Romans. Avitus was elected prefect of Gaul here in the fifth century.

By the eleventh century it was called by its present name, which means beautiful rocks. Houses were already clustering around its fortress. In the next century Simon de Montfort and the Count of Toulouse

---

Snow-capped ridges seen from just outside Beaucaire.

fought over the city. Beaucaire remained loyal to the count, and his gratitude brought the town many privileges, including the most important, the right to hold a great annual fair. This began on the eve of 21 July (the feast of St Mary Magdalene) and lasted a week – with the town filling up several days before and many visitors staying on for the following week as well.

The memory of this fair is one of the legendary aspects of Beaucaire. Peddlars, traders, merchants, sightseers, men and women simply longing for pleasure crowded into the town from every part of France and abroad – more than 100,000 of them. A flotilla plied the Rhône. Each street had its speciality: the present quai du Canal sold salt fish, the rue du Château wool. The Canal du Midi brought the fair and the town to a peak of prosperity, and it declined only with the coming of the railways and new patterns of commerce.

Frédéric Mistral celebrated the fair at Beaucaire as part of the essential rhythym of life that typified his beloved Languedoc culture:

'Under the pretext of trading,' he wrote, 'Beaucaire fair offered people the chance of experiencing for a fortnight, or even a month, the careless, exuberant free life of a Bohemian encampment. There you slept, in lodgings, in shops, on the counters, in the middle of the street, under the canopies of wagons, under the warm July stars.'

In his celebrated poem on the River Rhône Mistral also tells the tale of the dragon which lived here, a monster that one day snatched a laundress from the place Vieille. Every June a massive model dragon, with wings and fearsome teeth, is paraded through the streets breathing flames in memory of this episode.

Beaucaire gained its fair just as an anonymous Picardy troubadour was setting down the legend of Aucassin and Nicolette in verse and prose – a tale forgotten until a manuscript containing it was

---

The medieval château of Beaucaire, perched on a peak above the old city.

discovered in 1752. Aucassin, the Christian son of the Viscount of Beaucaire, falls in love with a young Saracen slave, captive daughter of the King of Carthage. Curiously enough, the name Aucassin is of Arabic origin, while Nicolette is French. After many disappointments and vicissitudes, the two lovers are united. The story has a happy ending, thanks chiefly, be it noted, to the girl's persistence and not to any particular effort on the part of Aucassin.

There is still a fair here from 21 to 27 July, held at the fair-ground by the river, next to the arena – for Beaucaire also has a Corrida boasting 'the best bulls and the best *razeteurs*'.

The Syndicat d'Initiative has had the excellent idea of putting little brown square plaques on the walls of notable buildings in Beaucaire, numbered in white, with little arrows pointing you on a tour that is described in a handy leaflet the Syndicat gives you free of charge. My advice is to ask for the French edition (or maybe a French and an English one), since the English translation is execrable.

If you don't fancy following such a detailed itinerary, do not miss the massive domed church of Notre-Dame-des-Pommiers, rebuilt by Jean-Baptiste Franque between 1734 and 1744. The marble font, high altar and pulpit are by Dominique Fossati of Marseille. There are actually two pulpits, with a marble pomegranate suspended from the main one. There are fine eighteenth-century paintings, and a superb organ.

Next to the church stand a few vestiges of the old romanesque cloister. And J.-B. Franque cleverly incorporated a long romanesque frieze high up on the south wall of the outside of his church, comparable to the lintel over the doors of the church at Saint-Gilles-du-Gard, telling the story of Holy Week. Whereas the carving at Saint-Gilles ends with Jesus on his way to death, here the story continues: Jesus is laid in his tomb, and then (insofar as I can make it out) three women come and find the tomb empty, Jesus having risen from the dead.

Beaucaire's charm derives as much from its arches and lovely doorways as from its fine buildings. Even so, walk south from Notre-Dame-des-Pommiers along the rue de l'Hôtel-de-Ville to look at the late seventeenth-century town hall. This is noble enough to have been attributed for many years to Mansart, but is in fact by the Nîmes architect J. Cubizol. The nicest place to admire it from is while sitting in the café opposite, itself a former sixteenth-century town house and for many years inhabited by the sisters of an Ursuline convent.

Then walk on, turning left at rue Eugène-Vigne. An eighteenth-century house on the corner was once the home of Franciscans. When the financier Jacques Coeur fell from grace in 1453, Charles VII condemned him to live with the friars. He escaped across the river and tried to take refuge with the pope, but he died *en route* to Rome. Further down rue Eugène-Vigne is the stern, lovely Franciscan church of Saint-Paul.

Walk from here to the top of rue Salengro from where mighty arcades lead into the place de la République. This attractive square boasts four plane trees and three cafés and is best seen in the evenings when the hanging lamps give it a romantic atmosphere. Along the rue de la République to the west is a splendid balconied house, with an ornate couple of seventeenth-century caryatids holding up the porch. And just north is the château of Beaucaire, which is worth visiting. From its gardens you can look out at the mighty château of Tarascon across the Rhône.

The D2 runs along the right bank of the Rhône to Villeneuve-lès-Avignon, through the little town of Aramon. The old château here was enlarged in 1553 (note the classical balustrades) and restored in the nineteenth century and there are many fine sixteenth- and seventeenth-century town houses. If you want to explore its eleventh-century church with an excellent classical portico, you will need to get the key from M. le Curé, whose presbytery is by the pharmacy in the town.

In the tenth century a Benedictine monastery stood isolated high on an island at Villeneuve-lès-Avignon, for the Rhône in those days flowed around both sides of the site. Then, in 1292, King Philippe the Fair decided to develop the spot as a new town

The *tour des masques* **guards an angle of fort Saint-André, Villeneuve-lès-Avignon.**

(Villeneuve). One of his plans was to tax the people of Avignon, on the left bank of the river. All that remains of his castle today is the square tower now named after him and built in 1302.

Then the popes came to Avignon. The cardinals, needing sumptuous homes for themselves outside the city, sought land at Villeneuve, and fifteen of them eventually possessed splendid palaces here. Cardinal Arnaud de Via, who instituted a college of twelve canons dedicated to the veneration of the Virgin Mary in Villeneuve, is buried in the powerful, fourteenth-century collegiate church of Notre-Dame.

Jean-Baptiste Franque built the church of Notre-Dame-des-Pommiers at Beaucaire between 1734 and 1744.

Left **The** *tricolore* **flutters from the balcony of the seventeenth-century town hall at Beaucaire.**

Above **The eighteenth-century rotunda, created by Jean-Baptiste Franque to shelter a statue of Christ on the way to Calvary, in the cloister of St John at the Carthusian monastery of Villeneuve-lès-Avignon.**

177

Drive along the river bank to see another château in much better condition – a fortress completely surrounded by battlements and built by Jean the Good and Charles V in the late fourteenth century. At the gates of fort Saint-André, as it is called, are a couple of seats where you can take a glass of Rhône wine and glare balefully, as the French monarchs must often have done, at the papal palace across the river.

In spite of occasional hostility between king and pope, the popes at Avignon also embellished the royal city of Villeneuve. The Carthusian monastery of the Val-de-Bénédiction here was founded by Pope Innocent VI (when he was still a bishop). The monastery today still has many of its quiet fourteenth-century buildings. And in 1362 the body of Innocent VI was placed in the monastery church, in a superb tomb which he himself had commissioned.

From Villeneuve-lès-Avignon drive west for 20 kilometres to Remoulins, which is only a short distance from the Pont du Gard, part of the aqueduct built by Agrippa to bring 300 litres of water daily for 45 kilometres from the River Gard to Nîmes. It is (to quote Paul MacKendrick's *Roman France*) 'one of the best preserved, most picturesque, and most famous sections of aqueduct in the Roman world'.

I find it frightening. I have only once climbed up to the top, 48.77 metres above the river, and tried to walk across it, on the slabs above the channel where the water once flowed. Children were running heedlessly along the unprotected stones. One brushed passed me and I almost fell off. Slowly I turned around and walked vertiginously back to *terra firma*.

These days I prefer to admire its three sets of arches from below: 35 small arches on the upper level; the second level with 11 larger arches; the bottom level spanning the river with only 6 arches. Blocks weighing 6 tonnes tower 40 metres above you. The conchitic limestone quarries nearby from which they came are still in use.

If you look carefully you will see that the Romans carved a huge phallus between two arches on the upper storey. (There are similar carvings on the Nîmes amphitheatre.) This symbol (which the Romans regarded as protection against bad luck) was prudishly transformed by Frédéric Mistral into a young hare (it does not look like one). He propagated the story that it was an offering to the devil, who had promised that the River Gard would never destroy the aqueduct if he could possess the soul of the first being that walked across it. The first being was a hare, thrown onto the bridge by a wily woman, and the devil in a rage hurled it against the upper arches, where you can see it to this day.

Or rather, you cannot.

You can swim in the river underneath the Pont du Gard (though I always need something on my feet, since the beach is pebbly). Then the road continues westwards to the delicious town of Uzès, with its feudal château and a recently discovered underground church that predates the eleventh century.

Racine's uncle lived here, and the dramatist stayed a year and a half, soliciting and failing to obtain an ecclesiastical living. The former bishops' palace, which had no welcome for Racine, boasts lovely turreted walls. The central place aux Herbes is charmingly irregular, with white stone arcades and a fountain.

The arcades continue along rue de la République. Turn right from here along rue Dampmartin for the seventeenth-century cathedral of Saint-Théodorit, built on the site of a pagan temple dedicated to Mars, the god of war. The interior is quaint, with a double clerestory, the first barred with fine wrought iron. The organ (built around 1660) is fantastic. And the church has a twelfth-century Italianate bell-tower, the only one in France. It looks like the tower at Pisa, save that it isn't leaning.

Next to the cathedral is the wildly decorated home of the eccentric Baron of Castile (he bought it in 1819 and started embellishing it almost immediately). The baron also married a girl thirty-eight years his junior and countered the mockery this provoked by giving her five children.

The massive Pont du Gard, built by the Romans to bring 300 litres of water daily to Nîmes.

Above In the early morning half-opened shutters suggest that a householder in the rue Jacques at Uzès is not yet fully awake.

Left The delicious town of Uzès, dominated by the eleventh-century tour Bermonde of its feudal château.

Right At Alès Louis Pasteur, who discovered the rabies virus in 1881, nobly offers a lady a helping hand, waving a piece of flax in the other, a microscope and pestle and mortar at his feet.

Uzès is 20 kilometres north of Nîmes, but if you choose to drive further to Alès, the route is packed with charming villages. It is worth pausing in Serviers-et-Labaume to glance at the seventeenth-century château and the romanesque church (partly rebuilt in the seventeenth century). Foissac has a pretty windmill. The church at Euzet burned down in 1703 but has been restored, and there are some old thermal baths here. At Monteils the Revolutionaries sold the Catholic church to the Protestants, so now it is a chapel. Méjannes-lès-Alès on the banks of the River Droude boasts a sixteenth-century church with tasteful nineteenth-century additions.

Alès, 50 kilometres northwest of Uzès, is today an industrial town, and though it does have a citadel by Vauban, a partly gothic former cathedral and an old château (now a museum with a bit of everything from prehistory to Dutch paintings), I should not mention it here but for the fact that Alphonse Daudet was extremely unhappy there. Family poverty meant he had to leave the *lycée* at Lyon without finishing his baccalaureate. He managed to find a job as an usher (a kind of supervisor of students) at the college at Alès. This proved to be purgatory and at one point he contemplated suicide. Instead he escaped into the Bohemian life of Paris.

Daudet later expressed the unhappiness of this time in his novel *Le Petit Chose* (*Little What's His Name*),

confessing in his memoirs, 'Yes, I was the one, and no other, *Little What's His Name*, who was forced to earn his living at sixteen years of age in that horrible position of usher, in the heart of a country of boorish mountaineers who used to insult me in their hard, coarse *patois*.'

I do not know whether the college where he worked still stands. You reach Vauban's fortress (which now houses the city archives) by driving up from the town hall past a statue of Louis Pasteur, who is helping a poor lady up off the ground with one hand and waving a piece of flax with the other. A plaque on the wall of the fortress records that Resistance leaders were tortured here in World War II. Nearby is a shady park, ideal for picnics.

It is a drive of 40 minutes or so from Alès to Nîmes. Look out for Vézénobres on your left – everything a medieval village should be, with twisting vaulted streets, parts of the old fortifications, ancient houses and gates, a couple of churches and no fewer than three châteaux. At Nîmes it is surely time to over-eat again, at least for once, like the old peasants that Daudet despised in his youth for hiding in a little corner of their fields, stupefied with food and drink and lying torpid, 'like boa constrictors roasting themselves in the sun'. Such sensations, Daudet sternly warned, 'have to be paid for later'. Of course they have, but the pleasure is worth the price.

Anduze, south of Alès, sheltering beneath hills rising from the River Gardon d'Anduze.

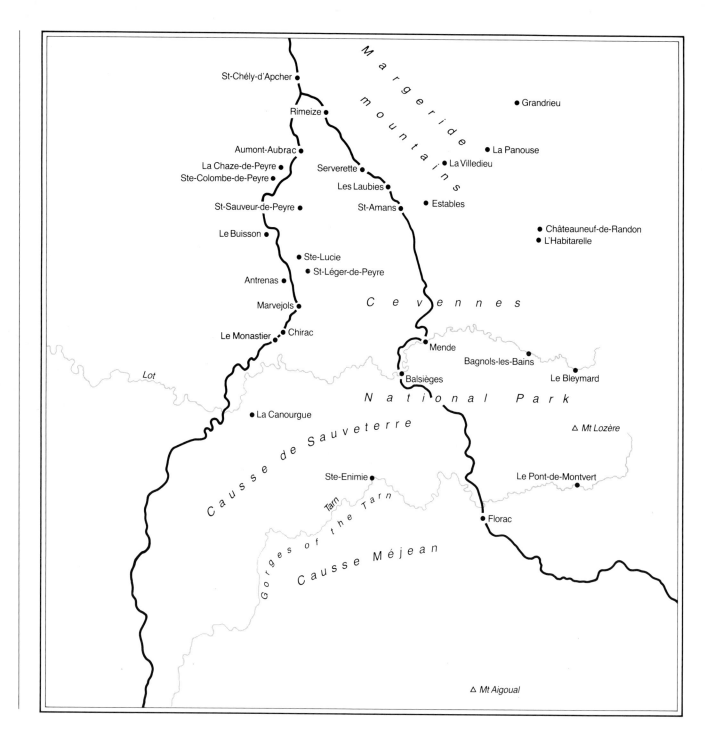

St-Chély-d'Apcher
Margeride mountains
Grandrieu
Rimeize
La Panouse
Aumont-Aubrac
La Villedieu
La Chaze-de-Peyre
Serverette
Ste-Colombe-de-Peyre
Les Laubies
St-Sauveur-de-Peyre
St-Amans
Estables
Le Buisson
Châteauneuf-de-Randon
L'Habitarelle
Ste-Lucie
St-Léger-de-Peyre
Antrenas
Cévennes
Marvejols
Le Monastier   Chirac
Mende
Bagnols-les-Bains
Balsièges
Le Bleymard
National Park
Lot
La Canourgue
△ Mt Lozère
Causse de Sauveterre
Ste-Enimie
Le Pont-de-Montvert
Tarn
Florac
Gorges of the Tarn
Causse Méjean
△ Mt Aigoual

6
The Spectacular Cevennes

*Mende – Sainte-Enimie – Le Monastier – Saint-
Chély-d'Apcher – Châteauneuf-de-Randon – the
Cevennes National Park – Le Pont-de-Montvert –
Florac – the gorges of the Tarn*

I first came to know the Cevennes through the chaplain to Spandau prison, Berlin. The one prisoner in Spandau is Rudolf Hess, Hitler's some-time aide, who quixotically flew to Britain to try to make peace during World War II, escaped the gallows at the Nuremberg trials, but was sentenced to life imprisonment.

Believing that it was high time to let Hess out, I did some BBC broadcasts about him. And I received a letter of thanks from the prison chaplain.

Now Spandau prison, Berlin, happens to be in the French military sector of that divided city. The chaplain to that prison happened to be the man who was military chaplain to the French occupying forces. He has a home in the Cevennes and (as you might expect in this part of France) he is a Protestant. We met in London. I grew to know him better. He told me about where he lives in France and urged me to visit the area. So I did – also relishing the notion of staying for next-to-nothing in his Cevennes home.

I found an exquisite, sometimes ravishingly beautiful area of France. Although included in the Languedoc, it is quite unlike any other part of this region. Officially known as the *département* of the Lozère, it is beautiful in part simply because it is so isolated. Nearly ninety per cent of the working population has something to do with the land, with raising sheep or with farming.

The Lozère is remarkable also because the countryside itself is astonishingly varied. The region is made up of quite distinct zones, each presenting the visitor with its own uniquely entrancing flavour. Southwest Lozère consists for the most part of high, chalky plateaux, pierced by ravines, often almost totally denuded of grass or trees. To the northwest are the volcanic Aubrac mountains, rising to 1470 metres in the peak of the Malhebiau. To the northeast and east two mountain ranges – the huge granite Margeride range and the Cevennes – combine in a vast expanse of fearsome ancient land, much eroded over countless centuries. The ridges of the Cevennes rise to two separate peaks, Mont Lozère (from which the *département* gets its name) at 1699 metres and the Aigoual at 1567 metres.

Thirdly, this region is virtually all countryside. Every prospect pleases and man is scarcely to be seen. Compared with the other *départements* of the Languedoc, Lozère has a tiny population, although it is roughly the same size as the others. Covering 5180 square kilometres, the population at the last census was exactly 80,234. By comparison, the population of Haute-Garonne, with Toulouse as its capital, is nearly 800,000, while Hérault, based on Montpellier, has a population of nearly 700,000.

Life is still hard, as it always has been for those who

have to scratch a living on these beautiful, bleak ranges. Nevertheless men and women have lived here for thousands of years. The caves in these rocks offered welcome shelter to neolithic man, and there are many prehistoric remains to be seen. A Celtic tribe know as the Gabales lived here, managing to adapt themselves to Roman rule. St Privat evangelized the Lozère in the third century and his Christian successors planted monasteries throughout the region. Picturesque villages, fifteenth- and sixteenth-century châteaux, ancient bridges and many fine markets — all of them still necessary to the life of the Lozère and its people — provide a land of enchantment for the tourist.

Start a first visit at Mende. Unlike the other great *département* capitals in this book, this is little more than a market town, but it is packed with charm and proud to be the *préfecture* of the Lozère. I like it better than Perpignan, or Albi, or Toulouse. It is totally unthreatening, altogether welcoming.

I arrived there late one summer as the sun was setting and took a coffee in a café on the west side of the cathedral. From where I was sitting I had a good view of the massive statue of the Christian boy from the Lozère, Guillaume de Grimoard, who became Pope Urban V. The setting sun illuminated the cathedral behind him, the warm stone between the spires a slightly deeper hue than the rest, the rose window still gorgeous even as it grew dark. And I marvelled at the way the whole west end seems to make architectural sense, even though the two belfries are so different, one squat and stern, the other gaily crocketed and fretted.

Saint Privat was martyred here. Pursued by barbarians he took refuge in a cave, but they discovered his hiding-place and killed him. His place of martyrdom became a centre of pilgrimage and his devout bones were housed in a little church. Privat's tiny church has become the crypt of the great cathedral, which was built over his tomb. It would be easy to miss it. One of the oldest crypts in the whole of France, it is entered by a miniscule entrance on the right-hand side of the cathedral, down some steps a third of the way from the west end towards the altar.

With such a powerful relic as the body of St Privat, the cathedral was a magnet for pilgrims, who invariably brought wealth with them. The bishops of Mende became rich and great men. They battled with the secular lords for suzerainty over the city and won; years later, in 1161, they gained recognition as lords of the whole region, then called Gévaudan.

The history of Mende cathedral fascinates me partly because well over a decade ago I became parish priest of a church in a part of England as deprived as the Lozère, and decided to restore the gothic building to its former beauty. Such a task costs money. I learned how you take risks, cut corners and finally come out on top. As I read about the way the bishops and canons of Mende had created the present exquisite cathedral, I realized that times had not changed. I do have to say, however, that they cut far more corners, and took many more risks than I ever dared. Still, the principle was the same. This is how Mende cathedral, as it stands today, was created — to the greater glory of God and with the aid of some devilish tricks.

Until the twelfth century it was an austere romanesque building, like most of the humble churches in the Lozère. A century later this lovely style had been superseded by the gothic architecture which was sweeping through France, and the canons of Mende cathedral wanted to transform their building. Alas, their bishop had scarcely any interest in their dreams. He was hardly ever in his cathedral anyway, since he was a great secular lord as well as a bishop. And the cost of rebuilding seemed beyond their means.

Their dreams, however, were shared by Guillaume de Grimoard, now the Benedictine abbot of Marseille. In 1362 this son of the Lozère became pope, and decided to build a new gothic cathedral for the diocese in which he was born.

His scheme for paying for it was brilliant, if slightly dubious, and involved a three-pronged plan. Guil-

The valley of the Langouyrou, northeast of Mende.

At Mende a hideous face guards the entrance to the administrative centre of the *département* of the Lozère.

laume, or Urban V as he now was, appointed the bishops of Mende. He decreed that any episcopal revenues which came in in the time between one bishop's transfer or death and the appointment of the next should go towards rebuilding the cathedral. The diocese then fell vacant. To make sure the money supply did not dry up, Urban simply postponed making a new appointment for nearly two years.

Secondly, many men of the Lozère owed the pope money. Urban allowed the cathedral canons to collect these debts and keep them. In this way the cathedral building fund received 4000 golden florins owed to Urban by a certain Gavin d'Apcher. The pope sent a further 6000 golden florins out of his own pocket.

Thirdly, knowing that the relics of the dead brought pilgrims to a great church (and therefore income),

Urban sent the cathedral what he believed was the head of St Blaise. He even gave the canons a far more precious relic: a splinter purporting to be from the very cross on which Christ was crucified. And he sent tapestries, jewels and vestments as well.

As a result, the canons were able to set to work rebuilding their cathedral. They engaged one of the great roving architects of the late thirteenth century, Pierre Morel, to supervise the whole building. Born in Majorca, Morel had built an abbey at La Chaise-Dieu. He had also been involved in the palace of the Duke de Berry and had worked on great buildings at Lyon and Avignon.

Stonemasons poured into Mende from all parts of France and Morel and his army of workers began on the nave at Mende in 1369. Quite unexpectedly, Pope Urban V died the following year. The work stopped, with only the nave completed; the choir had scarcely been begun. For the next eighty years Mende cathedral stood half rebuilt, the choir and nave separated by a wooden screen.

Most of the bishops of Mende seem not to have cared. The cathedral canons, who lived on the spot, cared very much and secretly began selling the jewels given to them by their late benefactor, taking care not to tell the bishop.

In 1452 work began in earnest on the choir. The two master-masons responsible were Pons Gaspar and his second-in-command Jean Duront. Duront came from the Auvergne, but passion for the new task so gripped him that he bought a house in Mende, and even gave cash of his own to help pay for the very project that was his livelihood. Duront lived and breathed for this great masterpiece and he is the man to be credited with the artistic achievement. His master Gaspar was not involved on a day-to-day basis and simply made visits to inspect the work.

Even the bishop was now fired with enthusiasm for the project, and gave some money. The laymen of Mende decided to remit some of the revenues from taxing wine to the cathedral. In 1467, the choir was at last finished.

Here then is a fascinating building about which we

know nearly every detail. Although both choir and nave are gothic they are separated by eighty years and this is reflected in their styles. The actual building work was completed remarkably quickly. The choir was constructed in fifteen years, the nave in an astonishingly short four.

One remarkable feature of Mende cathedral is that it has two belfries, one highly ornamented in a style quite different from everything else in this simple, unpretentious and lovely cathedral. The reason is that it was authorized by an Italian bishop.

For forty-five years the della Rovere family held the bishopric of Mende. One of them, bishop from 1478 to 1483, never once came here, simply pocketing the episcopal revenues. In 1483 he became Pope Julian II, but kept the bishopric in the family by appointing his nephew Clement to the see. Clement remained Bishop of Mende for twenty years, resigning just before his death to make sure that the bishopric passed to his brother François.

François had by now transformed the family name from della Rovere to the French, de la Rovère. He remained Bishop of Mende till his death in 1524. And he decided his cathedral needed a splendid belfry. At this the canons determined that they too would build another belfry, smaller than the bishop's, since they were poorer than he was. With scrupulous politeness, the leading canon was invited to lay the first stone of the bishop's belfry in 1509; the following year the canons invited the bishop's vicar-general to lay the first stone of their belfry.

The bishop's belfry is not only taller than the canons'; it is also far more ornate. Delicate ogival decorations appear half-way up its buttresses. A graceful balustrade runs across it and continues along the west end of the cathedral, pulling the architecture together, so to speak, but stopping when it reaches the canons' belfry.

Above, an elegant colonnade transports the new grace of the Italian renaissance to this gothic Lozère cathedral. Crowning it all, two bays higher, four arched buttresses support a tower with a slender, crocketed octagonal spire. The buttresses themselves carry smaller spires matching the great one.

Not counting the cross on top, the bishop's belfry rises 84 metres above the ground. The spiral staircase up to the tower has 244 steps. And again and again you can make out Bishop François de la Rovère's coat of arms – two branches of oak, with the bishop's mitre and episcopal cross – sculpted on the belfry, in case anyone might forget who donated this magnificent work of architecture. Since François also helped to pay for the canons' humbler belfry, a mere 65 metres in height, he had his coat of arms sculpted on that too.

Slowly the belfries were hung with bells, named after St Privat, Pope Julian, Bishop François de la Rovère, and the evangelists Matthew, Luke and John. For the three evangelists' bells 300 kilograms of metal was dragged by 180 mules from Lyon to Mende, the Archbishop of Lyon generously waiving his right to tax any goods passing through his diocese. A final bell named after St Mark was cast in 1523 at a cost of 400 livres.

Scarcely had this magnificent building been finished than the Protestants started to try to demolish it. The Huguenot leader Merle did so much damage in 1581 that for twenty years afterwards Mass could be said only in a little chapel by the bishop's belfry. The reign of Henri IV brought some peace and the king himself helped to pay for the restoration, though the canons could not afford to renew the old sculpted ornamentation inside the cathedral: the walls today are beautiful but strangely bare. But the cathedral authorities did finance the exquisite rose window at the west end, created in 1606 by an architect from Orléans, Pierre Léneville.

After that Mende seems to have been mostly left alone by despoilers. At the Revolution someone smashed the stained glass of the rose window; the glass replacing it, made in 1931, glows happily enough. And once inside, you don't really notice that the walls are not so richly ornamented as they might be, for the cathedral is furnished with sumptuous works of art. These are not all masterpieces, but together they provide a gleaming feast for the eyes.

Mathieu Merle's vandalism destroyed the old organ.

In 1653 the cathedral ordered another, with a monumental case designed by Jean Tiran of Nîmes. On the left-hand side you can make out an angel playing a serpent – only the joke is that it happens to be a real serpent, not a musical instrument! Another angel musician plays a xylophone. A mob set fire to the organ at the Revolution, but the cathedral canons restored it again.

Next to the organ, on the right, is the huge hammer of one of the massive bells, which cracked. And in the baptism chapel nearby you can see some delightful seventeenth-century wood-carvings that were once part of the cathedral rood screen. They depict such Old Testament scenes as God creating Adam, Noah making his ark and an immodest Potiphar's wife, trying to tempt Joseph, who makes a hurried getaway.

In the first chapel on the left as you go in are more splendid carvings. I am especially fond of the Annunciation, while the life and death of St Privat remind you why there is such a building here at all.

The choir stalls were carved in 1692, depicting the life of Jesus from birth to death. These carvings are far more sophisticated than the rest, though there are a few homely touches as well, particularly the scene of the flight into Egypt. Joseph carries the entire possessions of the Holy Family for all the world as if he were the head of a peasant family moving house.

Before leaving Mende cathedral, seek out the carving of the Black Virgin in the chapel of Notre-Dame-de-Mende. Sculpted out of extremely hard wood by the monks of Mount Carmel in the eleventh century, it reached Mende in the mid twelfth century, brought by Crusaders. Almost immediately it was endued with miraculous powers, especially when the canons discovered that it was reputed to contain some of the Virgin Mary's own hair and fragments of Christ's cross. One canon payed for no fewer than 206 votive candles to be burned all at the same time in front of the statue.

The Virgin stood in the place of honour on the high altar, but by extraordinary strokes of luck escaped the vengeful Huguenots and the Revolution. During the Wars of Religion an old woman was bold enough to ask one of Merle's followers to give her 'that old stump of wood' for her fire. When peace returned she brought the statue back.

At the Revolution the Virgin on the altar was displaced by the Goddess of Reason, in her Phrygian bonnet and short skirt, one breast naked. This time a pious woman hid the Black Virgin under her skirt, smuggled her out of the cathedral and brought her back when the troubles were over.

In the square to the south of the cathedral is a statue of a hero of the Lozère, the unsung genius Jean-Antoine Chaptal (1756–1832), a precursor of the French chemical industry. Twice a week (on Wednesdays and Saturdays) the locals erect stalls around him to sell fruit and inexpensive clothing.

The place de la République further down the hill has a fountain, and a bust in honour of Henri Bourrillon, mayor of Mende and organizer of the Resistance here in World War II. The Nazis deported him in 1944, and he died the following year. 'He died,' the inscription reads, 'in defence of liberty.'

Follow the rue de la République east from here to Les Halles, the market erected in 1900 beside the old market square, with stalls selling *charcuterie*, sweet pink and white onions, bread, chicken and cheese every Wednesday and Saturday.

The former Chapel of the Penitents, a harmonious seventeenth-century church, is now an entirely satisfying little museum of religious art. One of the finest treasures it contains is its own baroque reredos, which is displayed alongside very early printed Bibles (filled with tendentious translations designed to defend Catholicism against the Huguenots), immaculately chased chalices, insouciant cherubs, and vestments so richly embroidered as to make any connoisseur of needlework drool helplessly over them.

Mende is a labyrinth of ancient streets crammed with little statues and modern boulevards (the latter

The thirteenth-century gothic bridge of Our Lady crosses the River Lot at Mende.

set out on the former moat of the town), all perched over the River Lot, which is spanned by a thirteenth-century bridge.

Wherever you walk, sleepy buildings are rich in fascinatingly bizarre history. In the rue de l'Ange you come upon the former Carmelite convent, with its fourteenth-century porch; here too is a college of secular priests, curiously inhabiting the thirteenth-century Jewish synagogue.

Drive southwest from Mende, following the signs for Millau along the N88, until you reach Balsièges, dominated by a great peak known as the lion of Balsièges. The church at Balsièges is half romanesque, half gothic. The château dates from 1635.

For once I find the peak more fascinating than the church and château (especially as you cannot visit the latter). Its name derives from the slightly absurd habit that the French so frequently indulge in of giving rocks sentimental names (as in the Sidobre and the Grotte des Demoiselles) – erroneously suggesting that they look like beasts, or cheeses, or pulpits.

One lump of dolomite here does vaguely resemble a resting lion (if you half close your eyes when looking at it). Actually I have gazed and gazed at it close up, and it looks nothing like a lion. None the less, it is worth climbing up the gently sloping winding path to the top of the mountain just to savour the panoramic views from the top – a foretaste of what is to come in the country of the Camisards.

Another entrancing walk winds steeply upwards to the chapel of Saint-Théodore, a seventeenth-century pilgrimage church attached to the saint they call Tchaouzou hereabouts. You reach the path (or rather, track) just south of Balsièges along the N88, to the right of the old stone kilometre post numbered 75.

At this point you are already in the wild country of the Lozère, where prehistoric man felt at home, though for us there is still a frisson of fear at the impending savagery of the countryside. Most of the prehistoric sites – dolmens, tumuli and the rest – are north of Balsièges, but the finest dolmen lies 200 metres west of the town and makes me suspect that there is much more here for prehistorians and archaeologists to discover.

Drive south from Balsièges to Sainte-Enimie, through thickly wooded pine forests swooping down the mountainsides to the valley. Soon you are driving across the sparsely vegetated Causse de Sauveterre. A series of trembling hairpin bends leads down to a tourist trap that will never be spoiled, because there is nowhere else to build.

Sainte-Enimie lies in a deep valley, alongside the wide River Tarn. Here are tourist shops, canoes and a beach. Here also is medieval beauty.

Walk up the steep cobbled street from the river to the romanesque church. By any kind of historical logic, this church ought not to be romanesque. By the time it was built, in the thirteenth and fourteenth centuries, everyone else was experimenting with the new style we now call gothic. But here time had stood still. The apse at Sainte-Enimie (which I once had to look at for over an hour, when I inadvertently joined some nuns worshipping there and someone locked the doors) is as lovely a romanesque apse as I have seen (and there are 400 or so in the *département* where I have my home).

The church is filled with exquisite statues, none of them obtrusive, all of them treasures. My favourite is the fourteenth-century statue of Saint Anne, the grandmother of Jesus; she holds her daughter Mary, who has her divine offspring in her arms. Grand-mamma carries everyone.

I would very much like to know what people think of the three modern ceramics in the chapel to the left of the altar, supposedly representing the life of St Enimie, who lived from 604 to 637. Her short life-span was the result of loving God rather than men. Enimie was a beautiful girl and many sought her hand in marriage. All were rejected. To rid herself of such tiresome suitors, St Enimie begged God to take away her beauty. She contracted leprosy. After some months of this disease, she was instructed by an angel to bathe in a

The entrancing cobbled streets of Sainte-Enimie, in the spectacular Tarn gorge.

The coat of arms of Pope Urban V, over the door of the church at Le Monastier where he was ordained.

fountain. She did so, and after the third bath the leprosy vanished.

Now she had to fight her own libidinous self – represented in the medieval story and in one of the St Enimie ceramics as the devil. Her pure nature won, she renounced men, founded a convent here and died as a hermit, welcomed into the arms of her true spouse, Jesus.

I think I like the modern ceramic in which Constant de Mende depicts all this, save for the artist's decision to represent leprosy by a piece of sticking plaster on the saint's nose.

The way up to the delightful medieval village of Sainte-Enimie has been signposted by the Syndicat d'Initiative. It is lovely, with half-timbered houses, turrets, drinking fountains and little arches leading up

the hill as far as the ruined abbey. Here the chapter house is still intact, though completely bare.

The easiest way out of this land-locked medieval survival is to drive back in the direction of Balsièges and then follow the road signs towards La Canourgue. The Tarn gorge is stunningly deep, the rock strata fascinating. (I should add that the road signs D598 and D998 are here apparently interchangeable, whatever your map says.) The windmills of La Canourgue once ground corn but are now derelict. In Napoleon Bonaparte's time the town also earned its keep clothing the revolutionary and imperial armies. Today this quiet old place preserves its picturesque streets, its medieval and renaissance houses, its twelfth-century priory church, its archways and its ruined château and seems to live in its own unhurried world, as if the twentieth century were a long way ahead.

Take the N9 beyond the village to Le Monastier, just 13 kilometres away. There are many picnic spots in the valley of the Lot *en route*, with seats thoughtfully provided by the local authority.

The village of Le Monastier takes its name from a Benedictine monastery founded in 1062. The twelfth-century church here (embellished but by no means spoiled in the sixteenth century) is certainly worth stopping for, containing fine capitals and a stone pulpit of 1726. A notice says that Pope Urban V was ordained here and you can see his coat of arms under the arch over the door of the church.

This godly son of the Lozère, Guillaume de Grimoard, was born here in 1310, became a Benedictine monk and studied law at Paris and Avignon. The brilliant student was soon a professor, teaching his subject first at Montpellier and then at Avignon. The Benedictines spotted his talents as a leader, as well as his natural goodness, and they made him abbot of their community at Auxerre. Guillaume

Steps and geraniums in an old corner of La Canourgue.

was transferred from there to be abbot at Marseille.

In 1362 he was elected pope because, it is said, the Italian cardinals could not agree which of them should take this office and chose a French candidate as a compromise solution.

These were the years of the papal exile at Avignon, for Rome was a city of violence and godlessness. Grimoard, now Pope Urban V, decided to work for the reform of clerical abuses. He restrained the greed of his servants and stopped clergymen possessing several livings at once and serving none.

Urban V also agreed to an absurd and incompetent crusade against the Turks. And he longed to restore the papacy to Rome and to re-unite eastern and western Christendom. He succeeded in neither ambition although he did in fact reach Rome in 1369. Moreover, the Byzantine Emperor John V Paleologus came to kneel at his feet and renounce the eastern doctrines as heresy. Urban was elated. He called a Council at Rome to announce the reunion of the two divided branches of the Church. Foolishly, however, he refused to allow easterners to join the councils of the western church, still distrusting their orthodoxy. As a result, on 21 October 1369 the eastern Christians failed to turn up for the triumphal ceremony at Saint-Peter's, Rome.

Turbulent Rome was still a dangerous place for a pope. Riots forced Urban to flee to Viterbo, and then to seek refuge back in Avignon. He was also prompted to return to France by his hope of ending the Hundred Years War. He failed, and died suddenly in Avignon in 1370.

Five hundred years later Urban V was beatified, the only one of the Avignon popes ever to be officially dubbed saintly by the Catholic Church.

The second delightful fact about Le Monastier (for the British) is that Robert Louis Stevenson bought his donkey here in 1878. Stevenson had suffered two emotional blows. He had fallen in love with a Mrs

Sitwell, legally separated from her husband but – alas, from Stevenson's point of view – passionate for his friend Professor Sidney Colvin of the University of Cambridge. He had then met a woman ten years older than himself, an American named Fanny Osborne, whom he soon adored. To make matters impossible for Stevenson, she was married, and had children. For a while they were lovers. Then Fanny Osborne and her offspring returned to California.

Can one say that a broken heart may be restored in the Cevennes? Stevenson thought so. Off he went, and wrote his first masterpiece, *Travels with a Donkey in the Cevennes*. And soon, he wrote, he blessed God that once again he was 'free to wander, free to hope, and free to love'.

There is pathos in the book, especially when he blurts out his dream of a life that is 'the most complete and free' of all, living out of doors with the woman he loves. But the book also radiates humour, especially when Stevenson fights his recalcitrant and idle mule Modestine.

Le Monastier, Stevenson found, was 'notable for the making of lace, for drunkenness, for freedom of language, and for unparalleled political dissension'. Every citizen loathed, hated, decried and calumniated his neighbour. But everyone wanted to be kind and helpful to himself, a stranger. He bought his donkey from Father Adam, who had a name in the village for brutally mistreating the animal. Nevertheless, when he parted with Modestine, Stevenson tells us, 'It is certain that he shed a tear, and the tear made a clean mark down one cheek.'

On the way to Marvejols, 7 kilometres north, you pass through the village of Chirac, which boasts the most impressive dolmen in the whole region, a pre-Christian construction known (absurdly) as the Chapel of Our Lady. Protestants sacked the town in 1562 and set fire to its church, but Saint-Romain at Chirac is still recognizably romanesque and well worth pausing for.

Marvejols itself is twinned with Cockermouth in the Lake District of England. A citizen of Marvejols whom I met in a tavern declaimed some words which he said were by William Wordsworth:

Plump cows graze near Chirac.

Spindly-legged Henri IV outside the north gate of Marvejols.

'I wondered lovely, as a crowd,
    that floats on high, through Wales and hells,
till all at once I said aloud
    this is a host of daffodils.'

The effort was extremely impressive (ask any citizen in Cockermouth to recite a little Lamartine and you will see what I mean), so I have since that day had no qualms about listening to it a second and a third time. Surely he is waiting there now for my next visit, when we shall once again evoke the muse.

Marvejols is a magically walled city. As you enter, the gate seems to be about to fall down, but it has stood thus for six hundred years. In the thirteenth century the town belonged to the kings of Majorca. Bernat Sicard de Marvejols was a celebrated troubadour, singing sadly of the devastation brought by the Albigensian crusade here.

In the sixteenth century the Protestants found Marvejols a haven. Then the Duke de Joyeuse besieged the town with French Catholics and German mercenaries. Marvejols surrendered only when the duke promised to spare its defenders. He broke his promise and executed three-quarters of them.

Drive through the town and out through the northern gate where there is a comical modern statue of Henri IV by Émmanuel Auricoste. Can Henri IV possibly have supported himself on such spindly legs? He has been immortalized here because, although he nominally embraced the Catholic faith when he became king, he paid for the ramparts of Protestant Marvejols to be rebuilt.

On all three gates of Marvejols there are curious stone plaques, inscribed as if the gate itself were talking. The northern gate proclaims in French the joyful assertion that Marvejols rose like a phoenix from the flames owing to Henri IV. The two other gates also sing Henri's praises, this time in Latin. The gate of Théron proclaims:

'These walls were destroyed and razed, but the invincible Henri IV, father of our country, raised the town from the ashes and, bringing it back to its former state, thus restored one of France's premier towns.'

The southern gate has an equally banal message.

If you walk up the hill from Henri IV's statue you reach the church of Notre-Dame-de-la-Carce, which displays insipid modern stations of the cross by Louis Rigne, who was born here. They have been lent by the Museum of Modern Art, Paris. I dislike these boring stations of the cross very much and wish the Museum of Modern Art would be good enough to take them back.

Opposite the church of Notre-Dame-de-la-Carce is a war memorial that continually brings me up short, since as an insular Englishman I tend to think that all wars ceased in 1945 (in spite of military skirmishes

The splendid entrance to the old church of Marvejols.

since then). It commemorates the dead of France's last colonial wars: in Morocco, Tunisia and Algeria – young men who perished as recently as 1950 to 1952.

In my view Auricoste created a better statue for the place des Cordeliers to the southeast of the city walls, which represents the fearsome beast of Gévaudan. To portray the beast of Gévaudan as a wolf may or may not be accurate. If he was a wolf, as Robert Louis Stevenson wrote, he was the Napoleon Bonaparte of wolves. Between 1764 and 1767 the beast ranged the mountains and plains, slaughtering some hundred women and children altogether. Rewards were offered for its capture, and many wolves were shot. But the slaughter continued. Bloodthirsty murderer or animal with a taste for human flesh, the beast of Gévaudan lives on in the folklore of the Languedoc.

The road from Marvejols runs north to Saint-Chély-d'Apcher, but it is worth pausing in Sainte-Lucie on the way. A group of optimistic conservationists are trying to rehabilitate the wolf in a 4-hectare park here, in spite of the off-putting reputation of the beast of Gévaudan, and this sanctuary is open to visitors during the summer. There are also many unknown villages of outstanding beauty just off the main road. Antrenas sports a nineteenth-century château matched by a fine church of the same date. Perched on a basalt peak at Saint-Léger-de-Peyre to the east stands the romanesque church of Sainte-Lucie, no longer in use since the village also possesses a well-restored fourteenth-century one (as well as a ruined abbey).

Still further north, this time to the west of the N9, is Le Buisson, whose church is also nineteenth-century but whose great antiquity is proclaimed by more than fifty local menhirs. At Saint-Sauveur-de-Peyre nearby, the church is built out of granite and – as a stele proclaims – the local serfs were freed in 1261.

Directly northwest, on the other side of the N9, is the charming village of Sainte-Colombe-de-Peyre, with its pretty twelfth-century church. Drive from here along a little country road northeast to La-Chaze-de-Peyre, where you can see traces of Agrippa's Roman road and a romanesque church with a graceful octagonal belfry.

If you continue north from La-Chaze-de-Peyre and turn right along the D987 you come to the ancient town of Aumont-Aubrac, its old houses tiled in stone and its windmills a reminder of a scarcely abandoned economy. The romanesque convent chapel has a beautifully sculpted virgin presiding over the entrance and decent enough modern stained glass.

Saint-Chély-d'Apcher is 11 kilometres north of Aumont-Aubrac. It is a tiny medieval town, with old houses, a church that cannot make up its mind whether it wants to be classified as twelfth- or seventeenth-century, and an intriguing wayside cross, with a quaint fifteenth-century carving of the Lamb of God. The locals dub this 'the cross of the English'. It is hard to say why. Certainly the English besieged Saint-Chély-d'Apcher in 1362 and were repulsed by the defenders. But that (apart from invading the place as tourists) is all that the British people are responsible for. Such traditional names always have some reason behind them, but I have asked and read and asked and read again, and no-one seems to be able to explain this one.

From here you explore the Lozère further by driving southeast to Serverette, 17 kilometres away. The route passes through Rimeize, with its eleventh-century church and ancient bridge. The bishops of Mende decided Serverette was a pleasant enough place for their château and built the feudal fortress whose remains still dominate the town.

South of Serverette on the way to Saint-Amans is one of those precariously balanced rocks that I used to think were confined to the Sidobre until I began exploring more of the Languedoc. They call this one the rocher de Saint-Jean, though St John was clearly far less responsible for this bizarrely spectacular granite outcrop than centuries of rain. You also pass by Les Laubies, where one of the houses has an entrancing doorway sculpted in the thirteenth century and where

Sunset over the lac du Moulinet at Combettes north of Marvejols.

Left **Mourning the dead of World War 1 at Saint-Chély-d'Apcher.**

Above **The valley of the River Truyère, north of Serverette.**

Left The curious rock of Vanel (equally curiously known as the rock of St John) stands precariously between Serverette and Saint-Amans.

Above The rolling countryside of the Cevennes near La Villedieu.

there are several communal bread ovens (none of them, alas, in use today).

Saint-Amans boasts a church with impressive capitals and (I think) little else. Turn left in the village for the road to Estables (with its ruined twelfth-century château) and take the D59, D34 and then D5 northeast to Grandrieu. On the way you pass through La Villedieu, a village with its romanesque church set amidst forest, heather and broom. As if the rich romanesque legacy were not already overwhelming, a little further on La Panouse boasts its own twelfth-century priory church.

Grandrieu has a romanesque church that I like very much. It contains fourteenth- and fifteenth-century frescoes depicting the crucifixion, the Virgin Mary, St Bartholomew and St John. Don't miss its south doorway. And from here the D985 runs 20 kilometres south to Châteauneuf-de-Randon, built on a rocky ledge overlooking the crossroads. The English were ceded this strategic spot at the treaty of Brétigny in 1360, but in 1380 the famous Du Guesclin decided to take it back.

Bertrand du Guesclin was the greatest general of the Hundred Years War. By 1370, at the age of fifty, he was Constable of France, the most prestigious military position of the age. Again and again he cunningly refused to take on the English in set battle, waiting until he could defeat them by brilliant manoeuvre and stealth. As brave as any of his soldiers, he was twice captured in battle. The French king valued him enough to pay a ransom of 40,000 gold francs. By 1380 he was in his prime.

But at Châteauneuf-de-Randon on 13 July 1380 he unwisely drank from one of the coldest springs in the Languedoc. As a result this squat, thick-set dynamic military genius died of pneumonia or some similar ailment. A bronze nineteenth-century statue in the main square of the town depicts Du Guesclin in his glory. His body lies at Saint-Denis in Paris, but it was planned to bury him here. Just outside the town, at L'Habitarelle, is an empty mausoleum, with a recumbent statue of the dead commander, a replica of that at Saint-Denis.

The church bell at Grandrieu.

From Châteauneuf-de-Randon drive due south by way of the N88 and the D27 to a T-junction where you turn left for Bagnols-les-Bains. The Romans had a spa here and built an aqueduct. Today it boasts an entirely up-to-date thermal centre – a perfect spot for a rest-cure, on the banks of the River Lot and the edge of the Loubière forest.

Keep on east – the château of Tournel dominating the mountain top – to reach Le Bleymard, which lies at the foot of Mont Lozère, with its ski-slope and a hundred invigorating walks. The village itself is blessed with picturesque old houses, some of them roofed with the sliced stones known as *lauzes* rather than with tiles. In my view the little romanesque church of Saint-Jean is totally enchanting, standing in a field just across the road from the fortified priory with its sweet round tower.

From here the D20 runs south through the Cevennes National Park, where the only dull objects are the sheep: the birds, gorges, rock-formations and *causses* are sensational. This is a land of dolmens and menhirs, caverns and superb walks.

From Le Bleymard the road climbs beside the Lozère forest. There are thick woods of pine trees and ancient stone bridges. Then the trees disappear, giving way to barren rocks, with a few heathers and just the occasional pine. The route passes the Col de Finiels (1548 metres) and huge stones covered in green lichen. Willow-herb and the berries of rowan trees now give a dash of colour. Patches of meadows reveal attempts at cultivation.

By way of Finiels you reach Le Pont-de-Montvert. Here the lovesick Robert Louis Stevenson met a peasant girl called Clarisse who 'waited at table with a heavy placable nonchalance, like a performing cow'. He added that 'her great grey eyes were steeped in amorous langour', that 'her features, although fleshy, were of an original and accurate design' and that her figure was unworthy of her face – 'a case', as he put it, 'for stays'. I can vouch that there are still a few Clarisses in Le Pont-de-Montvert.

The blessed Guillaume de Grimoard lived in Château Grisac, now a ruin. A romanesque Catholic church and a fine Huguenot chapel now stand together here. And at Le Pont-de-Montvert a seemingly peaceful seventeenth-century bridge crosses the River Tarn, with no hint at the savagery of its past. At one end of the bridge is a habitable tower built for collecting tolls, which was turned into a prison for Protestants in 1702 by the archpriest Langlade du Chayla. These Protestants called themselves Camisards, a word that signifies 'attackers by night', but their warlike reputation was a recent one. Most of them were small farmers, cloth- and silk-weavers, vine-dressers and other such humble men and women, though some were people of substance and most of

Bertrand du Guesclin, commemorated in a statue at Châteauneuf-de-Randon, where he died in 1380 after drinking from an ice-cold spring.

them, even the poorest, valued education. Since the Edict of Nantes had granted them a measure of toleration, these Protestants had been amongst the king's most loyal subjects. On 6 September 1683 150 of their leaders had met at Colognac and published a declaration of their personal fidelity to Louis XIV.

Two years later Louis XIV revoked the Edict of Nantes. Soon Camisard pastors were being sent to the galleys. Other leaders sought exile. One of these was Pierre Jurieu, who had studied philosophy at Saumur and visited England and the Netherlands. In 1686, when in Amsterdam, he prophesied the fall of the French monarchy in 1689. He also roundly declared

Above The charming old complex of Le Bleymard.

Right The ridges of the Cevennes fading into the distance from near Le Bleymard.

Above **The toll-house on the seventeenth-century bridge at Le Pont-de-Montvert is where the Protestants, led by Esprit Séguier, trapped and killed the Catholic missionary Du Chayla in 1702.**

Right **The peaceful valley of the Mimente, outside Cassagnas, where the deposed Protestant leader Esprit Séguier was executed in 1702 by the Catholics.**

that: 'The right of princes to use the sword does not extend to matters of conscience.'

Initially the Camisards had tried to cope with persecution by passive resistance. Jurieu was now preaching that open revolt was lawful for Christians. His followers secretly disseminated copies of his works in the Cevennes and throughout the Languedoc. Believing that their time would come, many of the Camisards took to mystical prophesying, falling into spiritual ecstasies which stoked their courage.

The monarchy responded with greater and greater repression. Over three hundred children were imprisoned at Uzès, accused of prophesying. The Church appointed Du Chayla, a former Chinese missionary, as inspector of missions in the Cevennes. He regarded it as his duty to try to convert Camisards by systematic torture. At Le Pont-de-Montvert his house on the bridge became his torture chamber.

On 23 July 1702 a Camisard named Esprit Séguier, a wool-carder by trade, led a group of Protestant men and women to the house. Du Chayla's guards fired at them from the upper storey. Undeterred the Camisards broke in and freed the prisoners from the lower storey. Du Chayla and his companions leapt and lowered themselves from the upper windows to escape, but the archpriest broke his thigh and began to crawl away. Fifty-two Camisards stabbed him to death. Then they sang psalms by his corpse all night.

Esprit Séguier wanted to continue by massacring every Catholic priest in the Cevennes. Other Camisards deposed him as leader. The vengeance of the authorities brought out the genius of humble men and women, provoking the wives, daughters and mothers of Camisards to accompany their men into battle, acting as nurses and preparing food. At the age of eighteen a baker's son named Jean Cavalier commanded their southern army. He was a match for the Count de Broglie and three French marshals, defeating them all.

Cavalier made peace, on terms which allowed liberty of conscience, provided that the Camisards built no more chapels. Others refused such terms, demanding the restoration of the Edict of Nantes. Slowly they were put down. Three thousand men had risen against the oppressors. It took an army of 60,000 to defeat them. Altogether 12,000 Languedoc Camisards, including Séguier, were executed.

Drive from here west along the D998 by way of the sensationally spectacular gorges of the River Tarn. Green meadows by the river alternate with terrain on which nothing grows. After 18 kilometres, not far beyond a rocky fortress on your left, turn south into Florac, the capital of the Cevennes National Park, whose administrative offices are in the restored late sixteenth- and seventeenth-century château.

Florac is a busy, sparkling little town, though any undue noise is likely to be little more than that of men and women playing *boules*. The fury of the past (when, for example, the Huguenots demolished the Catholic church in 1561 and used its stones to build their chapel, only to see it razed by the Catholics a century later) is dissipated. Today there is a Catholic church built in 1833 and a Huguenot chapel of 1821. Walk under the shady plane trees of the esplanade and do not miss the fine doorway of the former Hôtel Narbonne-Lara, built in 1585. Here too are camp-sites, *gîtes* and quiet hotels.

Mende lies 39 kilometres northwest of Florac, by a lovely winding route that runs along both the Tarn and the Lot. Once I drove four friends back this way having done a little tour taking in Châteauneuf-de-Randon and Le Pont-de-Montvert. Remembering Du Guesclin's fate, we ordered a couple of bottles of the red wine called Saint-Saturnin. It had a curious, rich kind of dryness, as if fortified with the ancient dust of the martyr himself.

The Cevennes near Florac.